ROCKET MAN

ROCKET MAN

Elon Musk In His Own Words

EDITED BY JESSICA EASTO

AN AGATE IMPRINT

CHICAGO

Printed in the United States.

Rocket Man: Elon Musk In His Own Words
ISBN 13: 978-1-57284-214-4
ISBN 10: 1-57284-214-8
ebook ISBN 13: 978-1-57284-790-3
ebook ISBN 10: 1-57284-790-5
First printing: February 2017

10 9 8 7 6 5 4 3 2 1   17 18 19 20 21

B2 is an imprint of Agate Publishing. Agate books are available
in bulk at discount prices. For more information, go to
agatepublishing.com.

What I'm trying to do is to minimize future existential threats or take whatever action I can to ensure the future is good. I didn't expect these companies to succeed. I thought they would most likely fail.

—ELON MUSK, JANUARY 2016

TABLE OF CONTENTS

ENVIRONMENTALISM AND SUSTAINABLE ENERGY... 73

ENGINEERING, DESIGN, AND MANUFACTURE....... 105

INTRODUCTION

E LON MUSK WANTS TO CHANGE THE WORLD.

If researching this book has taught me anything, it's that Musk's unapologetic, unbridled ambition unsettles (or enrages) people at least as much as it inspires them. And yet it would be difficult to argue on objective grounds that the depth and breadth of his work are not changing the world in important ways.

Musk knew from an early age that he wanted to leave his home in South Africa for the United States—in his words, "the greatest country that's ever existed on earth"—in order to be in the best position to make a difference. In college, he decided the fields that were most likely to impact the future of humanity included the internet, space travel, and sustainable energy. Since then, he's been working to improve them one by one.

When eBay purchased PayPal (Musk's second internet company) in 2002, he walked away with a cool $180 million and promptly started pouring it into a seemingly insane venture: SpaceX, a private company that aims to "revolutionize space technology, with the ultimate goal of enabling people to live on other planets." Musk taught himself rocket science, became the company's chief designer, and set out to take the first step toward making life multiplanetary: reducing the cost of space travel. In the 14 years since then, Musk and his SpaceX team have transformed the way rockets are manufactured, reduced the cost of launches by millions of dollars, earned lucrative contracts from both commercial and government entities, and achieved numerous space-travel milestones, including the ability to launch and land (and hopefully reuse) an orbital rocket booster stage. The company's eyes are now set on Mars.

Meanwhile, in 2004, Musk joined the newly created Tesla Motors and made the company's mission "to accelerate the world's transition to sustainable energy" by making fully electric cars that are practical, fun, fast, beautiful, and available to everyone. First came the Roadster, which proved that an electric luxury sports car with suitable range could exist. Next came Model S, a luxury sedan, and then Model X, an SUV, both of which have been designed with safety as a top priority (Model S is the highest-scoring of any vehicle ever tested). When Tesla announced the long-awaited mass-market Model 3 in March 2016, it received close to 400,000 reservations in only two weeks.

Along the way, Tesla has revolutionized the manufacture of one of the most complex commercial products on earth, continuously innovated and improved notoriously complicated battery technology, gone toe-to-toe with the automotive industry and Big Oil, and invented and built practical systems for electric charging and power storage via Tesla Energy—which Musk hopes to build upon with the acquisition of SolarCity, a solar panel and installation company he's backed and advised since its creation in 2006. Between SolarCity, Tesla Energy, and Tesla Motors, Musk believes he has created a complete solution for all elements of sustainable energy: creation, storage, and transportation.

Musk is a maverick and a visionary, one with the rare ability to identify and navigate problems of almost incomprehensible scale and complexity—despite high barriers of entry and the risk of almost certain failure. Deeply involved with every aspect of his companies, he is primarily an engineer by desire and an entrepreneur and businessman by necessity. In the words of Bill Gates, "There's no shortage of people with a vision for the future. What makes Elon exceptional is his ability to make his come true."

Despite all of this, critics insist that Musk's companies are not successful: they don't make money; they don't meet their deadlines; their products are unsafe, untested, or unreliable; their ambitions are fundamentally flawed; and their CEO is a crazy, callous egomaniac who will not stop until he crushes his companies under the weight of his own hubris. I'll let Musk defend himself against these claims in his own words, but for now, it's worth noting that while scrutiny is certainly merited, the media's fixation on Musk's failures is often baffling, especially in light of his long list of accomplishments.

The truth is that even if all of his ventures folded today, Musk's efforts have already accelerated humanity's progress toward sustainable energy and multiplanetary civilization. He's exceeded expectations so many times that it's easy to forget the world in which he started, one with zero viable electric vehicle programs and outdated domestic launch vehicles that could no longer transport humans to space. With the sale of hundreds of thousands of Tesla Model 3s looming, other automotive companies are starting to take their own electric vehicle programs more seriously, most notably Chevrolet with its Chevy Bolt and Audi with its e-tron quattro. No aerospace company is closer to orbital rocket reusability than SpaceX—or to cost-effective rocket development, for that matter. A top executive at United Launch Alliance—Boeing and Lockheed Martin's space technology partnership and SpaceX's main US competitor—resigned in 2016 after admitting that ULA couldn't compete with SpaceX's launch costs.

In 2015, Musk cofounded OpenAI, a nonprofit dedicated to ensuring that artificial intelligence remains an open-source technology so that everyone has access to its benefits. Tesla's patents are also open source, which makes them available to anyone who wishes to benefit from them and underscores Musk's mission-driven, not money-driven, motives. Perhaps one of the more admirable (or inexplicable if you are on Wall Street) aspects of Musk's character is that he seems unconcerned with financial gain. That might be an easy stance for a multibillionaire to take, but Musk came close to bankruptcy after pouring most of his personal funds into SpaceX and Tesla during a rough time for both companies in 2008. Instead, as you'll see, he seems unambiguously dedicated to contributing solutions for the betterment of humankind and to ensuring that the future of humanity is a bright and inspiring one.

EARLY YEARS

....

Growing Up in South Africa

When I was a kid, I would just walk around reading books all the time. And I was also the youngest kid in my grade, so I was quite small. I was kind of a smart aleck. It was a recipe for disaster. I'd get called every name in the book and beaten up.

—*Time*, July 19, 2010

There was a level of violence growing up that wouldn't be tolerated in any American school. It was like *Lord of the Flies*. There were a couple of gangs that were pretty evil, and they picked their victims and I was one of them. I think part of what set them off was that I ended up sticking up for this one kid who they were relentless on. And that made me a target.

—*Vogue*, September 21, 2015

....

The Hitchhiker's Guide to the Galaxy

I had kind of an existential crisis, and I was reading various books trying to figure out the meaning of life . . . because it seemed quite meaningless. We happened to have some books by Nietzsche and Schopenhauer in the house, which you should not read at age 14. It's bad. It's really negative. But then I read *The Hitchhiker's Guide to the Galaxy*, which was quite positive.

—CHM Revolutionaries, January 22, 2013

It taught me that the tough thing is figuring out what questions to ask, but that once you do that, the rest is really easy. I came to the conclusion that we should aspire to increase the scope and scale of human consciousness in order to better understand what questions to ask. Really, the only thing that makes sense is to strive for greater collective enlightenment.

—*Bloomberg*, September 14, 2012

• •

Why Silicon Valley?

Whenever I'd read about cool technology, it'd tend to be in the United States or, more broadly, North America. . . . I kind of wanted to be where the cutting edge of technology was, and of course within the United States, Silicon Valley is where the heart of things is. Although, at the time, I didn't know where Silicon Valley was. It sounded like some mythical place.

—CHM Revolutionaries, January 22, 2013

• •

Education

One of the downsides of coming to a university in North America was that my father said he would not pay for college unless it was in South Africa. So I could have free college in South Africa or find some way to pay it here. Fortunately, I got a scholarship at UPenn, and so I did a dual undergraduate [degree] in business and physics at UPenn Wharton.

—CHM Revolutionaries, January 22, 2013

∙∙∙

College Dating

She said the first question I asked her was, "Do you ever think about electric cars?" She said no, she never does. It wasn't great. Recently [the line] has been more effective.

—CHM Revolutionaries, January 22, 2013

∙∙∙

Choosing a Career Path

When I was in college, I just thought, "Well, what are the things that are most likely to affect the future of humanity at a macro level?" And it just seemed like there would be the internet, sustainable energy, making life multiplanetary, and then genetics and AI. I thought the first three, if you worked on those, they were almost certainly going to be good, and then the last two are a little more dodgy.

—STVP Future Fest, October 7, 2015

∙∙∙

Starting an Internet Company

That summer of '95 . . . it seemed to me like the internet was going to have a big effect on humanity. I thought, "Well, I can either work on electric vehicle technology and do my PhD at Stanford and watch the internet get built or I could put my studies on hold and try to be part of the internet."

—*Who's Time*, April 22, 2014

It wasn't like, "Oh, I want to make a bunch of money." . . . With the internet, anyone who had a connection anywhere in the world would have access to all the world's information, just like a nervous system. Humanity was effectively becoming a superorganism and qualitatively different than what it had been before, and so I wanted to be part of that.

—STVP Future Fest, October 7, 2015

• •

1995 Funding Climate

I started in '95, and nobody had made any money on the internet. Even in Silicon Valley, we went to venture capitalists in '95, and they had sort of heard of the internet—most of them weren't even using it—and [they thought] even if the internet did become widespread, nobody would make any money on it. Then Netscape went public, and that kind of changed people's mind-set—at least from the standpoint of the greater fool theory: even if these internet companies can't make money, at least some fool is willing to pay a lot if they go public.

—Web 2.0 Summit, November 7, 2008

● ●

Zip2

I didn't have any money, so I thought we've got to make something that's going to return money very, very quickly. We thought the media industry would need help converting its content from print media to electronic, and they clearly had money. If we could find a way to help them move their media to the internet, that would be an obvious way of generating revenue. There was no advertising revenue on the internet at the time. That was really the basis of Zip2.

—lecture at Stanford University, October 8, 2003

● ●

X.com

I wanted to do another company with the internet because I thought we hadn't really reached the potential that we could have with Zip2. We had really sophisticated software—our software was at least comparable to what Yahoo! or Excite or others had. In fact, I thought in some ways, it was better. But because it was all filtered through these partners, it wasn't getting properly used. I wanted to do something that could be a more significant contribution to the internet. The initial thought was financial services because money is digital, it's low bandwidth—at the time, most people were on modems.

—CHM Revolutionaries, January 22, 2013

PayPal Beginnings

PayPal got started in late '98 to early '99, and it was a merger of two companies: X.com that I started and Confinity that Max [Levchin] and Peter [Thiel] started. We pooled our resources and tackled the problem [of online payments] together. We went from starting the company to less than 14 months later having a valuation of $500 million. These days, after you see things like the recent acquisition [of Instagram] by Facebook, you think, "Oh, well maybe that's not that great." But at the time, it was certainly like, "This is completely ridiculous."

—PandoMonthly, July 12, 2012

LEARNING AND LOGIC

•••

Best Teacher

The best teacher I ever had was my elementary school principal. Our math teacher quit for some reason, and he decided to sub in himself for math and accelerate the syllabus by a year. We had to work like the house was on fire for the first half of the lesson and do extra homework, but then we got to hear stories of when he was a soldier in WWII. If you didn't do the work, you didn't get to hear the stories. Everybody did the work.

—Reddit AMA, January 6, 2015

•••

Critical Thinking

Do you have the right axioms, are they relevant, and are you making the right conclusions based on those axioms? That's the essence of criticial thinking, and yet it is amazing how often people fail to do that. I think wishful thinking is innate in the human brain. You want things to be the way you wish them to be, and so you tend to filter information that you shouldn't filter.

—CLEAN-tech Investor Summit, January 19, 2011

First Principles Thinking

I do think a good framework for thinking is physics, you know, the first principles reasoning. What I mean by that is boil things down to their fundamental truths and reason up from there as opposed to reasoning by analogy. Through most of our life, we get through life by reasoning by analogy, which essentially means kind of copying what other people do with slight variations. And you have to do that, otherwise mentally you wouldn't be able to get through the day. But when you want to do something new, you have to apply the physics approach. Physics has really figured out how to discover new things that are counterintuitive, like quantum mechanics; it's really counterintuitive.

—TED Talk, February 27, 2013

Explaining the "Why"

A lot of kids are in school puzzled as to why they're there. I think if you can explain the "why" of things, then that makes a huge difference to people's motivation. Then they understand purpose.

—Khan Academy Chats, April 17, 2013

· ·

How to Learn

I do kinda feel like my head is full! My context-switching penalty is high, and my process isolation is not what it used to be. Frankly, though, I think most people can learn a lot more than they think they can. They sell themselves short without trying. One bit of advice: it is important to view knowledge as sort of a semantic tree—make sure you understand the fundamental principles, i.e., the trunk and big branches, before you get into the leaves/details or there is nothing for them to hang on to.

—Reddit AMA, January 6, 2015

· ·

Learning Something New

I never had a job where I made anything physical. I cofounded two Internet software companies, Zip2 and PayPal. So it took me a few years to kind of learn rocket science, if you will.

—*Wired*, October 21, 2012

I had to learn how you make hardware. I'd never seen a CNC machine or laid out carbon fiber. I didn't know any of these things. But if you read books and talk to experts, you'll pick it up pretty quickly. . . . It's really pretty straightforward. Just read books and talk to people—particularly books. The data rate of reading is much greater than when somebody's talking.

—in conversation with Bill Gates, Boao Forum
for Asia, March 29, 2015

• •

Necessity of a University Degree

I do agree with Peter [Thiel]'s point that a university education is often unnecessary. That's not to say it's unnecessary for all people. You probably learn the vast majority of what you're going to learn there in the first two years, and most of it is from your classmates. Because you can always buy the textbooks and just read them. No one is stopping you from doing that. . . . Now for a lot of companies, they do want to see the completion of the degree because they are looking for someone who's going to persevere and see it through to the end, and that's actually what's important to them. So it really depends on what somebody's goal is. If the goal is to start a company, I would say there's no point in finishing college. In my case, I had to, otherwise I would get kicked out of the country.

—SXSW Conference, March 9, 2013

Dedication to Learning

You can learn whatever you need to do to start a successful business either in school or out of school. A school, in theory, should help accelerate that process, and I think oftentimes it does. It can be an efficient learning process, perhaps more efficient than empirically learning lessons. There are examples of successful entrepreneurs who never graduated high school, and there are those that have PhDs. I think the important principle is to be dedicated to learning what you need to know, whether that is in school or empirically.

—lecture at Stanford University, October 8, 2003

Structured Learning

It shouldn't be that you've got these grades where people move in lockstep and everyone goes through English, math, science, and so forth from fifth grade to sixth grade to seventh grade like it's an assembly line. People are not objects on an assembly line. That's a ridiculous notion. People learn and are interested in different things at different paces. You really want to disconnect the whole grade-level thing from the subjects. Allow people to progress at the fastest pace that they can or are interested in, in each subject. It seems like a really obvious thing.

—SXSW Conference, March 9, 2013

Inventing Solutions

.. ınk I'm good at inventing solutions to problems. Things seem fairly obvious to me that are clearly not obvious to most people. And I'm not really trying to do it or anything. It just seems like I see the truth of things and others seem less able to do so.

—*Morning Edition*, August 9, 2007

The Truth

I care a lot about the truth of things and trying to understand the truth of things. I think that's important. If you're going to come up with some solution, then the truth is really, really important.

—AutoBild.tv, November 6, 2014

BUSINESS

• •

Starting a Business Is Not Fun

A lot of times people think creating companies is going to be fun. I would say it's not. It's really not that fun. There are periods of fun, and there are periods where it's just awful. Particularly if you're the CEO of the company, you actually have a distillation of all the worst problems in the company. There's no point in spending your time on things that are going right, so you only spend your time on things that are going wrong. . . . I think you have to feel quite compelled to do it and have a fairly high pain threshold.

—Khan Academy Chats, April 17, 2013

• •

Usefulness over Money

It's better to approach this [building a company] from the standpoint of saying—rather than you want to be an entrepreneur or you want to make money—what are some useful things that you do that you wish existed in the world?

—in conversation with Bill Gates, Boao Forum for Asia, March 29, 2015

• •

Profit as Motive

I think the profit motive is a good one if the rules of an industry are properly set up. There is nothing fundamentally wrong with profit. In fact, profit just means that people are paying you more for whatever you're doing than you're spending to create it. That's a good thing.

—Khan Academy Chats, April 17, 2013

• •

The Purpose of a Company

The ability to attract and motivate great people is critical to the success of a company because a company is a group of people that are assembled to create a product or service. That's the purpose of a company. People sometimes forget this elementary truth. If you're able to get great people to join the company and work together toward a common goal and have a relentless sense of perfection about that goal, then you will end up with a great product. And if you have a great product, lots of people will buy it, and then the company will be successful.

—AutoBild.tv, November 6, 2014

Compelling Product, Compelling Price

Fundamentally, if you don't have a compelling product at a compelling price, you don't have a great company.

—Inc. 5000 Conference, 2008

40 Hours a Week

You're not going to create revolutionary cars or rockets on 40 hours a week. It just won't work. Colonizing Mars isn't going to happen on 40 hours a week.

—*Vogue*, September 21, 2015

Creating a Productive Environment

I think it's incredibly important that you have an environment in general where people look forward to coming to work because it's just so much easier to work hard if you love what you're doing.

—2016 Tesla Annual Shareholders Meeting,
May 31, 2016

Staffing

A small group of very technically strong people will always beat a large group of moderately strong people.

—*Fast Company*, February 1, 2005

Interviewing Candidates

, just ask them to tell me the story of their career and some of the tougher problems that they have dealt with, how they dealt with those, and how they made decisions at key transition points. Usually that's enough for me to get a very good gut feel about someone, and what I'm really looking for is evidence of exceptional ability. Did they face really difficult problems and overcome them? . . . Usually the person who's had to struggle with the problem, they really understand it and they don't forget if it was very difficult. You can ask them very detailed questions about it, and they'll know the answer, whereas the person who was not truly responsible for that accomplishment will not know the details.

—AutoBild.tv, November 6, 2014

A Good Heart Matters

The biggest mistake in general that I've made—and I'm trying to correct for that—is to put too much of a weighting on somebody's talent and not enough on their personality. . . . It actually matters whether somebody has a good heart. It really does. And I've made the mistake of thinking that sometimes it's just about the brain.

—SXSW Conference, March 9, 2013

"Special Forces" Approach to Firing

I want to accentuate the philosophy that I have with companies in the startup phase, which is a sort of "special forces" approach. The minimum passing grade is excellent. That's the way I believe startup companies need to be if they're ultimately going to be large and successful companies. We'd adhered to that to some degree, but we'd strayed from that path in a few places. That doesn't mean the people that we let go on that basis would be considered bad—it's just the difference between Special Forces and regular Army. If you're going to get through a really tough environment and ultimately grow the company to something significant, you have to have a very high level of dedication and talent throughout the organization.

—Web 2.0 Summit, November 7, 2008

Choosing a CEO

It's really hard to find someone who can grow a company. Running a company in a steady state is much easier than growing a company.

—AutoBild.tv, November 6, 2014

CEOs and Their Technology

I'm head engineer and chief designer as well as CEO [at SpaceX], so I don't have to cave to some money guy. I encounter CEOs who don't know the details of their technology and that's ridiculous to me.

—*Smithsonian* magazine, December 2012

Are You a Good Boss?

I try to be a good boss most of the time—not all the time.

—Automotive News World Congress,
January 13, 2015

Competitors

We don't think too much about what competitors are doing because I think it's important to be focused on making the best possible products. It's maybe analogous to what they say about if you're in a race: don't worry about what the other runners are doing—just run.

—StartmeupHK Venture Forum, January 26, 2016

Encouraging Innovation

Establish an expectation of innovation, and the compensation structure must reflect that. There must also be an allowance for failure because if you are trying something new, necessarily there is some chance it will not work. If you punish people too much for failure, then they will respond accordingly, and the innovation you get will be very incrementalist. Nobody's going to try anything bold for fear of getting fired or being punished in some way. The risk-reward must be balanced and favor taking bold moves. Otherwise, it will not happen.

—Offshore Northern Seas, August 2014

There's no map. By its nature, it's unknown, which means you're going to make false moves. It must be OK to make false moves.

—in conversation with Bill Gates, Boao Forum for Asia, March 29, 2015

Interns

Interns are great because they don't know what's impossible.

—2016 Tesla Annual Shareholders Meeting, May 31, 2016

● ●

MBAs at SpaceX

I'd much rather promote someone who has strong engineering ability than so-called management ability. We do hire some MBAs, but it's usually in spite of the MBA, not because of it.

—MIT Aeronautics and Astronautics Centennial Symposium, October 24, 2014

● ●

The Problem with Professional Managers

Great things will never happen with VCs [venture capitalists] or professional managers. They have high drive, but they don't have the creativity or the insight. Some do, but most don't.

—*Inc.*, December 1, 2007

● ●

Pitfalls of "Process"

I don't believe in process. In fact, when I interview a potential employee and he or she says that "it's all about the process," I see that as a bad sign. The problem is that at a lot of big companies, process becomes a substitute for thinking. You're encouraged to behave like a little gear in a complex machine. Frankly, it allows you to keep people who aren't that smart, who aren't that creative.

—*Wired*, October 21, 2012

. . . .

Skip-Level Meetings

For a company, when it's very small, productivity grows quickly because of specialization of labor. Then productivity per person declines due to communication issues as the company gets bigger. As you have more and more layers through which communication has to flow, that necessarily imparts errors. Every time information flows from one person to another to another—even with the best of intentions—you have information loss. . . . To the degree that you can alleviate that by doing things like skip-level meetings, I think it's a good idea.

—Edison Electric Institute Annual Convention,
June 8, 2015

. . . .

Meetings Philosophy

The basic rule for meetings is that unless somebody is getting enormous value from the information they are receiving or they are contributing to the meeting itself, they should not be there. And we also have a rule that if somebody's in a meeting and finds that this meeting is not helping them in a meaningful way and they are not contributing to the meeting, they should just leave.

—Edison Electric Institute Annual Convention,
June 8, 2015

• •

Soliciting Feedback

Always solicit critical feedback, particularly from friends. Because, generally, they will be thinking it, but they won't tell you.

—SXSW Conference, March 9, 2013

• •

Why Companies Fail

[People] either have a strategy where success is not one of the possible outcomes—occasionally it's that. And then they don't change that strategy once that becomes clear, amazingly. Or they cannot attract a critical mass of technical talent, if it's in a technology-related thing. Or they run out of money before reaching a cash-flow-positive situation. That tends to be what occurs.

—*GQ*, December 12, 2015

• •

Coming Close to Failure

I certainly have lost many battles. So far, I have not lost a war, but I've certainly lost many battles . . . more than I can count, probably.

—*Who's Time*, April 22, 2014

We came very close to both companies not succeeding in 2008. We had three failures of the SpaceX rocket, so we were 0 for 3. We had the crazy financial recession, the Great Recession. The Tesla financing round was falling apart because it's pretty hard to raise money for a startup car company if GM and Chrysler are going bankrupt. . . . Fortunately at the end of 2008, the fourth launch, which was the last launch we had money for, worked for SpaceX, and we closed the Tesla financing round Christmas Eve 2008, the last hour of the last day that it was possible.

—STVP Future Fest, October 7, 2015

....

Failure in Silicon Valley

There are many more ways to fail than to succeed. Particularly for a rocket, there's a thousand ways the thing can fail and one way it can work. You could have a lot of rocket failures to explore all the ways in which it could fail. But I do think that one great thing about Silicon Valley is that failure is not a big stigma. It's like if you try hard and it doesn't work out, that's OK. You can learn from that and do another company, and it's not a big deal.

—STVP Future Fest, October 7, 2015

• •

Keys to Success

Start somewhere and then really be prepared to question your assumptions, fix what you did wrong, and adapt to reality.

—Vanity Fair New Establishment Summit,
October 2015

INNOVATION, TECHNOLOGY, AND THOUGHTS ABOUT THE FUTURE

· ·

Let Innovation Evolve

It's important to create an environment that fosters innovation, but you want to let it evolve in a Darwinian way. You don't want to, at a high level, at a gut level, pick a technology and decide that that's the thing that's going to win because it may not be. You should really let things evolve.

—in conversation with Bill Gates, Boao Forum for Asia, March 29, 2015

. . . .

Importance of New Entrants

In certain sectors, like automotive and solar and space, you don't see new entrants. There's not a lot of capital going to startups and not a lot of entrepreneurs going into those arenas. The problem is that in the absence of new entrants into an industry, you don't have that force for innovation. It's really new entrants that drive innovation more than anything. That's why I have devoted my efforts to those industries, and they are industries that require quite a bit of capital to get going.

—PandoMonthly, July 12, 2012

. . . .

State of Innovation Today

There is a lot of innovation going on. There's probably a few too many talented entrepreneurs in the internet space, and I think their talent actually would be better served in some other industries. But I don't think we are facing some sort of low innovation period.

—Code Conference, June 1, 2016

Government and Innovation

I don't think the government intends to stand in the way of innovation, but sometimes they can overregulate industries to the point where innovation becomes very difficult. The auto industry used to be a great hotbed of innovation at the beginning of the 20th century, but now there's so many regulations.

—CHM Revolutionaries, January 22, 2013

Disruptive Change

I do think it's worth thinking about whether what you're doing is going to result in disruptive change or not. If it's just incremental, it's unlikely to be something major. It's got to be something that's substantially better than what's gone on before.

—SXSW Conference, March 9, 2013

Be Useful

I don't think everything needs to change the world, you know. . . . Just say: "Is what I'm doing as useful as it could be?"

—STVP Future Fest, October 7, 2015

Whatever this thing is that you're trying to create, what would be the utility delta compared to the current state of the art times how many people it would affect? That's why I think having something that makes a big difference but affects a small to moderate number of people is great, as is something that makes even a small difference but affects a vast number of people.

—Y Combinator's "How to Build the Future" series, September 15, 2016

Internet

The most remarkable thing that we do have today is the internet and access to all the world's information from anywhere. Having a supercomputer in your pocket is, I think, something people wouldn't have predicted in *Back to the Future*.

—STVP Future Fest, October 7, 2015

AI Acceleration

I think AI is going to be incredibly sophisticated in 20 years. It seems to be accelerating. The tricky thing about predicting things when there is an exponential is that an exponential looks linear close up. But actually, it's not linear. And AI appears to be accelerating, as far as I can see.

—STVP Future Fest, October 7, 2015

OpenAI

It's not as though I think that the risk is that the AI would develop all on its own right off the bat. The concern is that someone may use it in a way that is bad, and even if they weren't going to use it in a way that is bad, somebody could take it from them and use it in a way that's bad. That, I think, is quite a big danger. We must have democratization of AI technology and make it widely available. That's the reason [we] created OpenAI.

—Y Combinator's "How to Build the Future" series, September 15, 2016

There's a quote that I love from Lord Acton—he was the guy who came up with, "Power corrupts and absolute power corrupts absolutely"—which is that "freedom consists of the distribution of power and despotism in its concentration." I think it's important if we have this incredible power of AI that it not be concentrated in the hands of the few.

—Code Conference, June 1, 2016

• •

Neural Lace

I think one of the solutions [to the threat of god-like external AI]—the solution that seems maybe the best one—is to have an AI layer. If you think, you've got your limbic system, your cortex, and then a digital layer—sort of a third layer above the cortex that could work well and symbiotically with you. Just as your cortex works symbiotically with your limbic system, a third digital layer could work symbiotically with the rest of you.

—Code Conference, June 1, 2016

Creating a neural lace is the thing that really matters for humanity to achieve symbiosis with machines.

—Twitter, June 4, 2016

· ·

Being a Cyborg

We're already a cyborg. You have a digital version of yourself or partial version of yourself online in the form of your e-mails and your social media and all the things that you do. And you have, basically, superpowers with your computer and your phone and the applications that are there. You have more power than the president of the United States had 20 years ago. You can answer any question; you can videoconference with anyone anywhere; you can send a message to millions of people instantly. You just do incredible things.

—Code Conference, June 1, 2016

· ·

Electric Transport

I think, actually, all modes of transport will become fully electric, with the ironic exception of rockets. There's just no way around Newton's third law.

—TED Talk, February 27, 2013

• •

Improving Battery Technology

I do think batteries are one of the hardest technology problems out there because there are so many constraints on creating a useful battery. So many super smart people have broken their pick on improving batteries. It usually ends up being, on average, about a 5 to 8 percent improvement per year in energy density and economics.

—AGU Fall Meeting Presidential Forum,
December 15, 2015

My top advice for anyone who says they've got some breakthrough battery technology is please send us [Tesla] a sample cell. Don't send us a PowerPoint. Just send us one cell that works with all appropriate caveats. That would be great. That sorts out the nonsense and the claims that aren't actually true. Talk is super cheap. The battery industry has to have more BS in it than any industry I've ever encountered. It's insane.

—Tesla Motors Q3 2014 earnings call,
November 5, 2014

....

Autonomous Driving

The reality is that autonomous systems will drive orders of magnitude better than people. In terms of accidents per mile, it'll be far lower. Technologically, I think it's about three years away for full autonomy.

—*GQ*, December 12, 2015

Owning a car that is not self-driving, in the long term, will be like owning a horse—you would own it and use it for sentimental reasons but not for daily use.

—BBC, January 11, 2016

....

Supersonic Electric Jet

Down the road, I'd love to work on something, which is a vertical takeoff and landing supersonic electric jet, and leverage what I've learned from SpaceX and from Tesla to try to make that happen.

—Living Legends of Aviation awards dinner, January 22, 2010

....

Flying Cars

Flying cars sound cool, but then they do make a lot of wind, and they are quite noisy, and the probability of something falling on your head is much higher.

—StartmeupHK Venture Forum, January 26, 2016

• •

Hyperloop

How would you like something that never crashed, is immune to weather, goes three or four times faster than the bullet train that's being built—it goes an average speed of twice what an aircraft would do, so you would go from downtown LA to downtown San Francisco in under 30 minutes. And it would cost you much less than any other mode of transport because the fundamental energy cost is so much lower. And I think we could actually make it self-powering.

—PandoMonthly, July 12, 2012

I sort of shot my mouth off and said I feel like I have an idea that would work, and it turned out that it didn't work. With a lot of iteration, I was able to come up with something where the physics hangs together and then published the paper and just said, "Look, anyone who wants to do this, that's great. Be my guest." Because I sort of have my plate full running Tesla and SpaceX.

—Code Conference, June 1, 2016

••

Tunnels

The fundamental problem with cities is that we build cities in 3-D. You've got these tall buildings with lots of people on each floor, but then you've got roads, which are 2-D. That obviously just doesn't work. You're guaranteed to have gridlock. But you can go 3-D if you have tunnels. And you can have many tunnels crisscrossing each other with maybe a few meters of vertical distance between them and completely get rid of traffic problems.

—StartmeupHK Venture Forum, January 26, 2016

••

Bogus Space Ventures

There are a couple of things that I think are pretty bogus. One is space mining, another is space solar power. If you calculate how much it costs to bring either the photons from space solar power back to Earth or the raw material back to Earth, the economics don't make sense.

—lecture at Stanford University, October 8, 2003

· ·

Space Entrepreneurs

If SpaceX and other companies can lower the cost of trasport to orbit and perhaps beyond, then there is a lot of potential for entrepreneurship at the destination. You can think of it like the Union Pacific Railroad. Before there was the Union Pacific Railroad, it was really hard to have commerce between the West Coast and the East Coast. It would go by wagon or a really long sailing journey, but once there was the transport, then there were huge opportunities.

—International Space Station R&D Conference,
July 7, 2015

· ·

Orbital Synchronization

You can only go there every two years because the orbital synchronization of Earth and Mars is about every two years. But I think it would be an interesting way for the civilization to develop. People would meet each other and be like, "What orbital synchronization did you arrive on?"

—*Vogue*, September 21, 2015

. . . .

Price of Interplanetary Humanity

I think the first journeys to Mars are going to be very dangerous. The risk of fatality will be high— there's just no way around it. I would not suggest sending children. It would be, basically: Are you prepared to die? If that's OK, then you're a candidate for going.

—International Astronautical Congress,
September 27, 2016

. . . .

Simulated Reality

Hope we're not just the biological boot loader for digital superintelligence. Unfortunately, that is increasingly probable.

—Twitter, August 3, 2014

. . . .

Loss of Technology

What a lot of people don't appreciate is that technology does not automatically improve. It only improves if a lot of really strong engineering talent is applied to the problem. . . . There are many examples in history where civilizations have reached a certain technology level and then have fallen well below that and then recovered only millennia later.

—International Astronautical Congress,
September 27, 2016

TESLA

Master Plan

Build sports car
Use that money to build an affordable car
Use *that* money to build an even more affordable car
While doing above, also provide zero emission elec-
    tric power generation options
Don't tell anyone.

> —"The Secret Tesla Motors Master Plan (Just between
> You and Me)," August 2, 2006

Genesis of Tesla

I really didn't want to be CEO of two companies. I
tried really hard not to be, actually. I actually told
AC Propulsion, "Look, if you're not going to do
this [develop a high-end electric car], I'm going to
create a company to do this." And they said, "Well,
there are some other guys who are also interested
in doing that, and you guys should combine efforts
and create a company." And that's basically how
Tesla came together.

> —CHM Revolutionaries, January 22, 2013

• •

Money Is Not Motivation

Our goal is not to become a big brand or to compete with Honda Civics. Rather, [it's] to advance the cause of electric vehicles. So we're just going to keep making more and more electric cars and driving the price point down until the industry is very firmly electric.

—Khan Academy Chats, April 17, 2013

We think it actually is going to make a difference to the world if we transition to sustainable transport sooner rather than later. We're not doing this because we thought it was a way to get rich.

—Automotive News World Congress,
January 13, 2015

What Tesla's motivation is is to make electric transport as affordable as possible. That is what informs all of our actions. So if we do something, and we charge for this or charge for that, it is not because we want to make things more expensive, it's because we can't figure out how to make it less expensive.

—2016 Tesla Annual Shareholders Meeting,
May 31, 2016

Mistakes

We'd made so many mistakes in the beginning of Tesla that we basically had to recapitalize the company almost completely in 2007. Almost every decision we made was wrong.

—Baron Investment Conference,
November 6, 2015

The decisions we've made along the way reflect that, really, we always try to do the right thing. We really care about that. When we make mistakes, it's just because we were being foolish or stupid or whatever, but it's really always made with the right motivations. We say the things that we believe even when sometimes those things we believe are delusional.

—2016 Tesla Annual Shareholders Meeting,
May 31, 2016

World's Worst Demo

I remember in the early days giving a test ride to Larry Page and Sergey Brin, who I've known for a long time, and there was some bug in the system and, damn it, the car would only go 10 miles an hour. And it was like, "I swear, guys, it goes a lot faster than this." But they were kind enough to put a little investment into the company nonetheless, despite the world's worst demo.

—2016 Tesla Annual Shareholders Meeting, May 31, 2016

Tesla IPO

Tesla's initial public offering was $226.1 million, which critics felt was unduly high.

When people see who's investing in the IPO, it's the smartest, most long-term-thinking investors in the market. It's really an amazing set of investors. So I think it's just worth noting that the smartest money in the world is betting on Tesla. They must have a reason for doing so.

—*Bloomberg*, June 29, 2010

Investors and Ideology

When we were in public even, I said, "Look, Tesla has a strong ideological motivation, so they shouldn't invest if they disagree with that." So they knew from the beginning—I've always been very clear about that. But as long as we make compelling products, I think Tesla will do OK. We shouldn't do OK just because the competition failed. We should do OK because we make good cars. That's the only reason.

—*Dagbladet Børsen*, September 23, 2015

Stock Price

If I ever do a tweet or a public announcement, it's got nothing to do with the stock price. What concerns me is I don't want customers thinking something that's wrong. For long-term investors in Tesla, the short-term fluctuations are not important. We cater our actions and our announcements to the long-term investors in Tesla. Those are the ones we really care about. The people that are in it just to speculate and then are out the next day—we feel about them about the same way they feel about us: we don't care.

—Automotive News World Congress,
January 13, 2015

●●

Tesla Bailout

A lot of people think that Tesla was bailed out by the federal government or something like that. This is not true. We were bailed out, but by Daimler, not by the government.

—2016 Tesla Annual Shareholders Meeting,
May 31, 2016

●●

Reality Check

The only two American car companies in history that have not gone bankrupt are Ford and Tesla.

—2016 Tesla Annual Shareholders Meeting,
May 31, 2016

●●

Don't Cut Corners

Creating a new car company is extremely difficult and fraught with risk, but we will never be a company that by our action does, or by our inaction allows, the wrong thing to happen just to save money.

—"Response to Mercury News Article, Entitled
'The Hidden Workforce Expanding Tesla's Factory,'"
May 16, 2016

Building Trust

We believe in doing deals where both parties benefit, and, when there is an asymmetry or underperformance on our part, interpreting that in the other party's favor. . . . Our goal in doing so is to build long-term trust. If people know that we will not take advantage of them and aspire to fairness, even at our own expense, then they are much more likely to want to work with us in the future.

—"The House Always Wins," November 21, 2014

No Model Years

We have a philosophy of continuous improvement. Every week, there are approximately 20 engineering changes made to the car. . . . Other manufacturers tend to bundle everything together in a model year. In our case, it's a series of rolling changes, so [the] model year doesn't mean as much.

—Tesla Motors Q3 2015 earnings call,
November 3, 2015

• •

8-Year, Infinite Mile Warranty

If we truly believe that electric motors are funda-mentally more reliable than gasoline engines, with far fewer moving parts and no oily residue or com-bustion byproducts to gum up the works, then our warranty policy should reflect that.

—"Infinite Mile Warranty," August 15, 2014

• •

Acquisition of Fremont Factory

Tesla purchased a 5.5-million-square-foot factory in Fremont, California, from Toyota in 2010.

Tesla was so tiny at the time. Imagine you are this little group and somebody says there is this giant alien dreadnought that you can have for pennies on the dollar, and you have no idea how it works. And you're like, "Where are the controls? How do you use this thing?"

—Baron Investment Conference, November 6, 2015

· ·

Fire Risk

A gasoline tank has 10 times more combustion energy than our battery pack. Moreover, the Model S battery pack also has internal firewalls between the 16 modules and a firewall between the battery pack and passenger compartment. This effectively limits the fire energy to a few percent that of a gasoline car and is the reason why Dr. Shibayama was able to retrieve his pens and papers from the glove compartment completely untouched after the recent fire (caused by a high speed impact with a tow hitch). It is also why arsonists tend to favor gasoline. Trying to set the side of a building on fire with a battery pack is far less effective.

—"The Mission of Tesla," November 18, 2013

∙∙

Range Transparency

At Tesla we pride ourselves on transparency with customers and feel that range is a topic where this is particularly important. There is not a single fixed range for any given vehicle or battery. The simple reality is that driving range can and will vary by a large amount depending on how you operate the vehicle and external factors such as wind and elevation change. The goal of providing this information is so that the driver/customer has a more complete picture of what can affect his/her range and are in a better position to predict and control the outcome.

—"Model S Efficiency and Range," May 9, 2012

∙∙

Unprofitability

I think an important point that seems to be lost by most people is that if Tesla were just making the sports car and doing our powertrain supply business, we would be profitable as a company. However, we're expanding massively—we're talking about expanding by 3,000 percent in the space of two to three years. It's just not possible for the company as a whole to be profitable with that rate of expansion. That's the reason for the unprofitability. It's not some fundamental flaw in the Tesla business.

—*Bloomberg*, June 29, 2010

Deliveries versus Demand

I think sometimes its difficult to interpret these [delivery] numbers because we will make cars in batches. For three weeks, we'll just make cars for Asia, and then we'll switch to cars for Europe, and then we'll switch to cars for the US. And then those will get delivered in waves. So people see huge differences in deliveries from one month to the next and assume that somehow consumers are going through these wild gyrations in their interest in the car. It's actually got nothing to do with that. It's just when the boat left.

—Automotive News World Congress,
January 13, 2015

Supply Chain Woes

Things move as fast as the least lucky and least competent supplier. Any natural disaster you care to name—all of those things have happened to our suppliers. The factory has burned down, there's been an earthquake, there's been a tsunami, there's been massive hail, there's been a tornado, the ship sank, there was a shoot-out at the Mexican border—no kidding. That delayed trunk carpet.

—Code Conference, June 1, 2016

● ●

On Accusations of High Attrition

The Wall Street Journal *had recently written an article suggesting that Tesla was losing talent.*

Is there a company that exists that has not lost talent on earth anywhere? Well, of course not. There's attrition at every company. What matters is, what's the longevity of key executives and personnel at the company? Do they stay there a long time or is there a lot of turnover? Our turnover is less than the industry average, not higher. That's why the article was so ridiculous. They use the example of the Tesla general counsel where they said Tesla had, in the course of one year, three general counsels. That sounds like a lot—except whenever an executive position changes in a year, you have two.

—Automotive News World Congress,
January 13, 2015

● ●

Safety

In designing the Model S and the Model X, safety was our absolute paramount goal. I felt like, obviously, my family will be in the car, my friends' families—if I didn't do everything possible to maximize safety and something went wrong, I couldn't live with myself.

—Baron Investment Conference,
November 6, 2015

Driver Responsibility

We're going to be quite clear with customers that the responsibility remains with the driver. We're not asserting that the car is capable of driving in the absence of driver oversight. That will be the case at some point in the future—like maybe five or six years from now, I think we will be able to achieve true autonomous driving where you could literally get in the car, go to sleep, and wake up at your destination. But in order to do that, you have to have fully redundant systems. Everything's got to be redundant so that any one system breaking does not result in an accident, and you also have to prove that out over millions of miles of driving.

—Bloomberg, October 10, 2014

Partial Autonomy Now

I should add a note here to explain why Tesla is deploying partial autonomy now, rather than waiting until some point in the future. The most important reason is that, when used correctly, it is already significantly safer than a person driving by themselves and it would therefore be morally reprehensible to delay release simply for fear of bad press or some mercantile calculation of legal liability.

—"Master Plan, Part Deux," July 20, 2016

Autonomous versus Manual Driving

Tesla will argue for autonomous driving, but we're not going to argue against manual driving. I believe people should have the freedom to choose to do what they want to do. And, yes, sometimes those things are dangerous, but freedom is important. If people want to drive, even if it's dangerous, they should be allowed to drive.

—Tesla Motors Q1 2016 earnings call,
May 4, 2016

Missing Deadlines

Well, I do have an issue with punctuality.

—Automotive News World Congress,
January 13, 2015

When I cite a schedule, it is actually the schedule I think is true. It's not some fake schedule that I don't think is true. It may be delusional—that is entirely possible, and it's happened from time to time. But it's never some knowingly fake deadline, ever.

—Code Conference, June 1, 2016

• •

Creating Deadlines

I want to emphasize that the July 1 date is not a date that will actually be met. It is an impossible date. However, it is a date we need to hold ourselves to internally and we need to hold suppliers to. But it is an impossible date because there are six, seven thousand unique components in the Model 3, and that would assume that all of them arrive on time. Just like a college term paper, there are always late term papers, but you still have to have a deadline, and it needs to be real and one with consequences if the deadline is not met.

—Tesla Motors Q1 2016 earnings call, May 4, 2016

• •

Mission

Our goal when we created Tesla a decade ago was the same as it is today: to accelerate the advent of sustainable transport by bringing compelling mass market electric cars to market as soon as possible. If we could have done that with our first product, we would have, but that was simply impossible to achieve for a startup company that had never built a car and that had one technology iteration and no economies of scale. Our first product was going to be expensive no matter what it looked like, so we decided to build a sports car, as that seemed like it had the best chance of being competitive with its gasoline alternatives.

—"The Mission of Tesla," November 18, 2013

● ●

Low Volume, High Price (Roadster)

What was unique about the Roadster was it was the first really great electric car. And before the Roadster, people thought an electric car would be slow and ugly and low range and have bad performance. And we had to break that mold. It was incredibly important to show that that wasn't true.

—Model 3 unveiling event, March 31, 2016

● ●

Mid Volume, Less-High Price (Model S)

It was rated by almost every group as the best car in its year and by *Consumer Reports* as the best car ever. The reason for that is not just to achieve some superlative in cars but to show what an electric car can do—because nobody believed that an electric car could do this.

—Model 3 unveiling event, March 31, 2016

● ●

Mid Volume, Less-High Price (Model X)

The revenue from the Model S and the X is what's needed to develop the Model 3. . . . It costs billions of dollars. So the S and the X are what pay for that Model 3 development.

—Model 3 unveiling event, March 31, 2016

. . . .

High Volume, Affordable Price (Model 3)

I want to emphasize that even if you buy no options at all, this will still be an amazing car. You will not be able to buy a better car for $35,000—or even close—even if you get no options.

—Model 3 unveiling event, March 31, 2016

. . . .

Model 3 Preorders

Model 3 racked up almost 400,000 preorders in two weeks.

It was quite surprising actually. We didn't do any advertising. There was no guerrilla marketing or anything. It was just basically like, yeah, we're going to have this webcast. There were only about 1,000 people in the audience. It really caught us by surprise. But I think when you have a product that really resonates with customers, the word of mouth grows like wildfire.

—Code Conference, June 1, 2016

••

Tesla Energy

Today, Tesla introduces Tesla Energy, a suite of batteries for homes, businesses, and utilities fostering a clean energy ecosystem and helping wean the world off fossil fuels. Tesla is not just an automotive company, it's an energy innovation company. Tesla Energy is a critical step in this mission to enable zero emission power generation.

—Tesla Energy press kit, April 30, 2015

••

Next Generation of Tesla Stationary Power Storage

What I'm highly confident of is that the next generation of stationary storage is head and shoulders above anything else that I've even heard announced as future plans from other companies. Now we've just got to build those damn things.

—Tesla Motors Q2 2016 earnings call,
August 3, 2016

．．

Gigafactory

At the Gigafactory, what we're doing is consolidating the production of the pack all the way from the raw materials, so there are literally [rail] cars coming in from the mines, and then out come completely finished battery packs. This has actually never been done before, for batteries at least. What we're able to do in this process is massively improve the cost of the cells in the packs. Because today . . . the raw material, that molecule from the mine, is doing an around-the-world trip, like, three times. It's really crazy.

—Baron Investment Conference,
November 6, 2015

The Tesla mission is to accelerate the transition to sustainable energy. I would say it's incredibly important that we do that. It matters to the world, it matters if it happens sooner or later, it matters if it happens at scale. And that's what the Gigafactory is about. It's about being able to make enough electric cars, enough stationary battery packs, that it actually moves the needle from a global carbon production perspective—so that it actually does really change the world. It has to be big because the world is big.

—remarks at Gigafactory grand opening,
July 29, 2016

....

Lithium Ion Batteries

The lithium is actually 2 percent of the cell mass. It's like the salt in the salad. It's a very small amount of the cell mass and a fairly small amount of the cost. It sounds like it's big because it's called *lithium ion*, but our batteries should be called *nickel graphite* because it's mostly nickel and graphite.

—Code Conference, June 1, 2016

....

Recycling Batteries

All of the battery packs for Tesla are currently recycled. There are recycling centers in North America and Europe and Asia. It kind of makes sense because you can just think of the battery packs as really high-quality ore. It's way better to mine a battery pack than rocks.

—AGU Fall Meeting Presidential Forum,
December 15, 2015

....

Tesla Watch

No longer will you need to rudely examine your phone to read text messages. Now you can politely stare at the tiny screen on your wrist without anyone noticing. This is in no way a competitive response to what some other company is doing.

—"Announcing the Tesla Model W," April 1, 2015

••

Apple

Yo, I don't hate Apple. It's a great company with a lot of talented people. I love their products and I'm glad they're doing an EV [electric vehicle].

—Twitter, October 9, 2015

••

Bioweapon Defense Mode

When the car is operating at maximum capability . . . we can't even detect any viruses or bacteria or spores. It's like zero come through. So if there's ever an apocalyptic scenario of some kind, hypothetically, you just press the Bioweapon Defense Mode button—this is a real button. We're trying to be a leader in apocalyptic defense scenarios.

—Model X unveiling event, September 29, 2015

••

Ludicrous Mode

It seemed ludicrously fast. And I like *Spaceballs* as a movie. So we named it "ludicrous mode" for that reason. I mean, I thought it was funny—maybe not everyone thinks it's funny, but I thought it was funny. I mean, it's memorable. I think people are gonna remember "ludicrous speed" more than they're gonna remember that it's, like, 2.8 seconds zero to sixty. And our competitors, they usually don't have a sense of humor, so I think that's a differentiator.

—*GQ*, December 12, 2015

. . . .

Open-Source Patents

Tesla Motors was created to accelerate the advent of sustainable transport. If we clear a path to the creation of compelling electric vehicles, but then lay intellectual property landmines behind us to inhibit others, we are acting in a manner contrary to that goal. Tesla will not initiate patent lawsuits against anyone who, in good faith, wants to use our technology.

—"All Our Patent Are Belong to You,"
June 12, 2014

Technology leadership is not defined by patents, which history has repeatedly shown to be small protection indeed against a determined competitor, but rather by the ability of a company to attract and motivate the world's most talented engineers.

—"All Our Patent Are Belong to You,"
June 12, 2014

Zero-Emission Credits

Zero credits were because you have all this toxic gas coming out of gasoline cars in close proximity to each other and hurting people's health. That's where the zero credits actually come from. Any manufacturer can acquire zero credits by making zero-emission vehicles. Again, it's a level playing field. If we're able to sell zero-emission credits, it's simply because some other manufacturer doesn't want to make zero-emission vehicles. This is not some special handout for Tesla. This existed decades before Tesla. To those companies, I would say, "Hey, why don't you make zero-emission vehicles?"

—Automotive News World Congress,
January 13, 2015

Retail Locations

Our stores are designed to be informative and interactive in a delightful way and are simply unlike the traditional dealership with several hundred cars in inventory that a commissioned salesperson is tasked with selling. Our technology is different, our car is different, and, as a result, our stores are intentionally different.

—"The Tesla Approach to Distributing and
Servicing Cars," October 22, 2012

• •

Sales Philosophy

[Our salespeople] are not on commission and they will never pressure you to buy a car. Their goal and the sole metric of their success is to have you enjoy the experience of visiting so much that you look forward to returning again.

—"The Tesla Approach to Distributing and Servicing Cars," October 22, 2012

• •

Service Philosophy

The best way to experience service is, of course, not to experience service.

—"Creating the World's Best Service and Warranty Program," April 26, 2013

I have made it a principle within Tesla that we should never attempt to make servicing a profit center. It does not seem right to me that companies try to make a profit off customers when their product breaks.

—"To the People of New Jersey," March 14, 2014

••

Pitfalls of Auto Dealers

Existing franchise dealers have a fundamental conflict of interest between selling gasoline cars, which constitute the vast majority of their business, and selling the new technology of electric cars. It is impossible for them to explain the advantages of going electric without simultaneously undermining their traditional business. This would leave the electric car without a fair opportunity to make its case to an unfamiliar public.

—"The Tesla Approach to Distributing and Servicing Cars," October 22, 2012

••

Potential Auto Dealer Partnerships

Some of the car dealer groups have been fairly negative in attacking Tesla. We're obviously not going to work with them. Just to be clear. If you've been a jerk to us, we're not going to turn around and try to do a partnership later. That would be crazy.

—Automotive News World Congress, January 13, 2015

• •

Focus

It is super important that Tesla stay focused on the goal of accelerating the advent of sustainable transport and sustainable energy. There are a lot of things that we could do that would be all these awesome social goods, but if we divide our energies over many social goods, we risk accomplishing none of them. We've got to stay focused on this fundamental good that we're trying to achieve as the primary thing, and then once we are over the hump—in particular, once we have a mass-market, affordable electric car that's great—then I think we can start to try to do other things, but we really need to stay focused on that goal for now.

—2015 Tesla Annual Shareholders Meeting,
June 9, 2015

• •

1 Million Cars by 2020

That's my best guess. If we're at a half million in 2018, and there's roughly 50 percent-ish growth from there, then it's probably around a million in 2020. I think it is actually feasible—maybe not advisable but feasible—to do it with just Fremont and the Gigafactory. We actually believe that Fremont and the Gigafactory could scale to a million vehicles. Whether that's actually wise is a separate question. It's going to make sense to do localized production at least on a continent basis. Otherwise, your logistics costs end up being quite extreme.

—Tesla Motors Q1 2016 earnings call, May 4, 2016

ENVIRONMENTALISM AND SUSTAINABLE ENERGY

....

Geosciences

It's quite surprising how little people know about geosciences, even pretty straightforward stuff like the carbon cycle. I mean, I've had conversations with quite smart and well-read people who don't understand that there's a surface carbon cycle, but if you dig stuff up from deep underground and add it to the surface carbon cycle, that fundamentally changes the chemical equilibrium of the surface of the Earth. And they're like, "Wow, really?"

—AGU Fall Meeting Presidential Forum,
December 15, 2015

Climate Change

The question isn't "Can you prove that we're making the planet warmer?" but "Can you prove we're not?" And you can't.

—*Smithsonian* magazine, December 2012

One should have a healthy skepticism of things in general, and from a scientific standpoint, you always look at things probabilistically, not definitively. A lot of times, if somebody's a skeptic in the science community, what they're really saying is that they're not sure that it's 100 percent certain that this is the case. But that's not the point. The point is to look at it from the other side and say, "What do you think the percentage chance is of this being catastrophic for some meaningful percentage of the Earth's population? Is it greater than 1 percent? Is it even 1 percent? If it is even 1 percent, why are we running this experiment?" We're playing Russian roulette [with the atmosphere], and as each year goes by, we're loading more rounds in the chamber.

—CHM Revolutionaries, January 22, 2013

• •

Elon Does Not Hate Hydrocarbons

I don't have any fundamental dislike of hydrocarbons. I simply look at the future and say, "What is the thing that will actually work?" And using a non-renewable resource obviously will not work.

—Offshore Northern Seas, August 2014

• •

Future of Oil and Gas

In the future, we'll look back—and by "future," I'm not talking about super far in the future; I'm talking about toward the end of the century—we will look back on gasoline-powered cars the same way we look back on coal: as a sort of quaint anachronism that's in a museum.

—Offshore Northern Seas, August 2014

There are time extensions on the game, but the game is going to come to an end. That should be absolutely certain—obviously, frankly. . . . If you're in nonrenewables, you're stuck in a room where the oxygen is gradually depleting, and then outside, it's not. You want to get out of that room. The ones that get out of the room sooner will be better off.

—Offshore Northern Seas, August 2014

• •

Transition from Fossil Fuels

I'm probably a little less alarmist than some: I think the danger is actually further off than is sometimes thought. But, at the same time, the solution is also very far off because the amount of electric vehicles needed to make a difference is hundreds of millions. And it takes a long time for an industry this big to change.

—*Telegraph*, August 4, 2007

• •

Conservation

If we don't have sustainable energy generation, there's no way that we can conserve our way to a good future. We have to fundamentally make sustainable energy available.

—presentation at Université Paris 1 Panthéon-Sorbonne, December 2, 2015

Best and Worst Cases of Delaying Transition to Sustainable Energy

If we wait, if we delay the change, the best case is simply delaying that inevitable transition to sustainable energy. This is the best case if we don't take action now. . . . The only thing we gain by slowing down the transition is just slowing it down. It doesn't make it not occur. It just slows it down. The worst case, however, is more displacement and destruction than all the wars in history combined.

—presentation at Université Paris 1 Panthéon-Sorbonne, December 2, 2015

De Facto Gasoline Subsidies

Every gasoline or diesel car that's going down the road has a de facto subsidy on it. People sometimes don't appreciate that. Whenever something is burning fossil fuels, it has a de facto subsidy. It's a subsidy of the public good. They're spending the carbon capacity of the oceans and atmosphere, not to mention the sulfur and nitrous oxides that are emitted, as it turns out, in greater quantities than regulators were told.

—2016 Tesla Annual Shareholders Meeting, May 31, 2016

• •

Carbon Tax

I'm generally a fan of minimal government interference in the economy—the government should be the referee but not the player, and there shouldn't be too many referees. But there is an exception, which is when there's an unpriced externality, such as the CO_2 capacity of the oceans and atmosphere. When you have an unpriced externality, then the normal market mechanisms do not work, and then it's government's role to intervene in a way that's sensible. The best way to intervene is to assign a proper price to whatever the common good is that's being consumed.

—CHM Revolutionaries, January 22, 2013

• •

Carbon Tax Opponents

This is being fought quite hard by the carbon producers, and they're using tactics that are very similar to what the tobacco industry used for many years. . . . Even though the overwhelming scientific consensus was that smoking cigarettes was bad for you, they would find a few scientists that would disagree, and then they would say, "Look, scientists disagree." That's essentially how they would try to trick the public into thinking that smoking is not that bad.

—presentation at Université Paris 1 Panthéon-Sorbonne, December 2, 2015

Solar Power

Something most people know, but don't realize they know, is that the world is almost entirely solar powered already. If the sun wasn't there, we'd be a frozen ice ball at 3 degrees Kelvin. The sun powers the entire system of precipitation. The whole eco-system is solar powered.

—TED Talk, February 27, 2013

One square kilometer is a million square meters. And there's one kilowatt per square meter of solar energy. So on one square kilometer, there is a giga-watt of solar energy. . . . You could power the entire United States with about 150 to 200 square kilometers of solar panels. The entire United States. Take a corner of Utah. There's not much going on there. I've been there.

—Offshore Northern Seas, August 2014

• •

China's Progress with Solar Panels

I think what China's doing in the solar panel arena is awesome because they're lowering the cost of solar power for the world. They have these huge gigafactories that they created out in the Chinese desert with a ton of funding from the Chinese government. So it's like a giant donation from the Chinese government. Like, "Thanks, that's awesome." . . . I think a good rule of thumb is, don't compete with China with a commodity product. You're really asking for trouble in that scenario.

—SXSW Conference, March 9, 2013

• •

The Hard Part of Solar Power

The hard part of solar power is not the panel. It's actually the whole system. It's basically designing something that's going to fit on a particular rooftop . . . then you've got to mount the system, you've got to wire it up, you've got to connect the inverters to the grid, you've got to do all the permitting. It's a bunch of thorny, unglamorous, stupid problems, but if somebody doesn't optimize them, they're still going to cost a ton of money. And a lot of them are not fun problems. They're not exciting problems to optimize, but they are the problems that actually matter in the cost of solar power.

—SXSW Conference, March 9, 2013

••

SolarCity

What SolarCity really is, is a giant distributed utility. And it's working in partnership with the house and business and in competition with the big monopoly utility. I mean, I think it's literally power to the people.

—SXSW Conference, March 9, 2013

••

SolarCity Acquisition

Now that Tesla is ready to scale Powerwall and SolarCity is ready to provide highly differentiated solar, the time has come to bring them together.

—"Master Plan, Part Deux," July 20, 2016

In order to solve the sustainable energy question, we need sustainable energy production, which is going to come primarily in the form of solar—overwhelmingly in the form of solar, in my view. Then combine that with stationary storage and an electric vehicle, and you have a complete solution to a sustainable energy future. Those are the three parts that are needed, and those are the three things that I think Tesla should be providing.

—press teleconference on Tesla acquisition of SolarCity, June 22, 2016

It's quite difficult to create an integrated product if you're forced to be at an arm's length and be two different companies. If we give a special deal to SolarCity, and SolarCity is not part of Tesla, then why are we doing that? We can do that if SolarCity is part of Tesla; we can't do it if SolarCity is a separate company.

—press teleconference on Tesla acquisition
of SolarCity, June 22, 2016

∙∙∙

What the World Needs

This is what the world needs. This is the ultimate solution for Earth. That's what we're talking about here. Solar power, stationary storage, electric cars— this is Earth's solution. We're going to try to make that happen as fast as possible, and the fundamental good of SolarCity and Tesla will be measured by the degree to which we accelerate that transition.

—press teleconference on Tesla acquisition
of SolarCity, June 22, 2016

What People Can Do

At the end of the day, the governments respond to popular pressure. If you tell politicians that your vote depends on them doing the right thing with climate change, that makes a difference. If they're having a fundraising event or a dinner pary or whatever and at every fundraising event and every dinner party, somebody's asking them, "Hey, what are you doing about the climate?," then they will take action. I think you have tremendous power. You have the power to make the change. We definitely can't beat the oil and gas industry on lobbyists. That would be a losing battle. Exxon makes more profit in a year than the value of the entire solar industry in the United States. If you take every solar company in the United States, it's less than Exxon's profit in one year. There's no way you can win on money. It's impossible.

—presentation at Université Paris 1 Panthéon-Sorbonne, December 2, 2015

Whenever you have the opportunity, talk to your politicians. Ask them to enact a carbon tax. We have to fix the unpriced externality. I would talk to your friends about it and fight the propaganda from the carbon industry.

—presentation at Université Paris 1 Panthéon-Sorbonne, December 2, 2015

SPACEX

••

A Small Fortune

When people ask me why I started a rocket company, I say, "I was trying to learn how to turn a large fortune into a small one."

—*Discover* magazine, September 8, 2005

••

Idea for SpaceX

I was trying to figure out why we'd not sent any people to Mars. Because the obvious next step after Apollo was to send people to Mars. . . . I discovered actually that NASA had no plans to send people to Mars or even really back to the moon.

—Khan Academy Chats, April 17, 2013

• •

Mars Oasis

I started with a crazy idea to spur the national will. I called it the Mars Oasis missions. The idea was to send a small greenhouse to the surface of Mars, packed with dehydrated nutrient gel that could be hydrated on landing. You'd wind up with this great photograph of green plants and red background— the first life on Mars, as far as we know, and the farthest that life's ever traveled. It would be a great money shot, plus you'd get a lot of engineering data about what it takes to maintain a little greenhouse and keep plants alive on Mars. If I could afford it, I figured it would be a worthy expenditure of money, with no expectation of financial return.

—*Wired*, October 21, 2012

• •

A Nation of Explorers

What I thought, really, was that we'd lost the will to explore, that we'd lost the will to push the boundary, and in retrospect, that was actually a very foolish error. Because the United States is a nation of explorers. The United States is a distillation of the human spirit of exploration. . . . But people need to believe that it's possible and that it's not going to bankrupt them.

—SXSW Conference, March 9, 2013

Reducing the Cost of Spaceflight

I said, OK, let's look at the first principles. What is a rocket made of? Aerospace-grade aluminum alloys, plus some titanium, copper, and carbon fiber. And then I asked, what is the value of those materials on the commodity market? It turned out that the materials cost of a rocket was around 2 percent of the typical price—which is a crazy ratio for a large mechanical product.

—*Wired*, October 21, 2012

I came to the conclusion that there wasn't really a good reason for rockets to be so expensive and that they could be a lot less. Even in an expendable format, they could be less, and if one could make them reusable, like airplanes, then the cost of rocketry would drop dramatically, the cost of space travel would drop dramatically.

—CHM Revolutionaries, January 22, 2013

The Goal of SpaceX

The goal of SpaceX is to revolutionize space travel. The long-term goal is to establish Mars as a self-sustaining civilization as well as to just kind of have a more exciting future.

—*hitRECord on TV*, February 1, 2014

● ●

Historical Context

If we continue upon the Apollo program and get to Mars and beyond, that will seem far more important in historical context than anything else we do today. The day multiplanetary species come about, things like the Soviet Union will be forgotten or merely remembered by arcane historical scholars. Things like the invasion of Iraq won't even be a footnote.

—*Pennsylvania Gazette*, November 4, 2008

● ●

Reasons to Make Life Multiplanetary

The probable life span of human civilization is much greater if we are a multiplanet species as opposed to a single-planet species. If we are a single-planet species, then eventually there will be some extinction event, either from humans or some natural thing. Now is the first time in the history of Earth that the window has opened, where it's possible for us to extend life to another planet. It's been four and a half billion years—it's a long time. That window may be open for a long time, and hopefully it is, but it may also be open for a short time. So I think the wise move is to make life multiplanetary while we can.

—AGU Fall Meeting Presidential Forum, December 15, 2015

I think it's also one of the most inspiring and interesting things that we could try to do. It's one of the greatest adventures that humanity could ever embark upon. Life has to be about more than solving problems. If all that life is about is solving problems, why bother getting up in the morning? There have to be things that inspire you, that make you proud to be a member of humanity.

—press conference on SpaceX's commitment to develop fully reusable rockets, September 29, 2011

•••

Success

I'm not saying we'll do it [become multiplanetary], to be sure. The odds are we *won't* succeed. But if something is important enough, then you should do it anyway.

—*GQ*, December 31, 2008

•••

First Order of Business

Our first order of business is to defeat the incumbent, old school rocket companies. Lockheed. Boeing. Russia. China. If this is a chess game, they don't have much of a chance.

—*Smithsonian* magazine, December 2012

• •

Problems with Aerospace Firms

One [problem] is the incredible aversion to risk within big aerospace firms. Even if better technology is available, they're still using legacy components, often ones that were developed in the 1960s. . . . Everyone is trying to optimize their ass-covering.

—*Wired*, October 21, 2012

Second, there's this tendency of big aerospace companies to outsource everything. That's been trendy in lots of industries, but aerospace has done it to a ridiculous degree. They outsource to subcontractors, and then the subcontractors outsource to sub-subcontractors, and so on. You have to go four or five layers down to find somebody actually doing something useful—actually cutting metal, shaping atoms. Every level above that tacks on profit—it's overhead to the fifth power.

—*Wired*, October 21, 2012

. . . .

Cost versus Reliability

Many times we've been asked, "If you reduce the cost, don't you reduce reliability?" This is completely ridiculous. A Ferrari is a very expensive car. It is not reliable. But I would bet you 1,000-to-1 that if you bought a Honda Civic that that sucker will not break down in the first year of operation. You can have a cheap car that's reliable, and the same applies to rockets.

—*Fast Company*, February 1, 2005

. . . .

Competing in Space

Speed for a rocket is always going to be roughly the same. The convenience and comfort is going to be about the same. Reliability has to be at least as good as what's been done before—otherwise people won't use your rockets to launch multihundred-million-dollar satellites—but there's not going to be much improvement there. So you're really left with one key parameter against which technology improvements must be judged, and that's cost.

—*Wired*, October 21, 2012

· ·

Competitive Advantage

In terms of our competitiveness, it mostly comes down to our pace of innovation. Our pace of innovation is much, much faster than the big aerospace companies or the country-driven systems. This is generally true. If you look at innovation from large companies and from smaller companies, smaller companies are generally better at innovating than larger companies. It has to be that way from a Darwinian standpoint because smaller companies would just die if they didn't try innovating.

—MIT Aeronautics and Astronautics Centennial Symposium, October 24, 2014

· ·

Aerospace versus Commercial Suppliers

Generally, we find if you want something cheap, fast, and it's probably going to work, then you should use a regular commercial supplier. If you want something that's expensive, takes a long time, and might work, use an aerospace supplier.

—International Space Development Conference, May 4, 2006

Blue Origin, Boeing, and Lockheed Partnership

It's certainly a good compliment. If all your competitors are banding together to sort of attack you, that's a good compliment, I think. A very sincere compliment.

—*Countdown to the Closing Bell*, September 17, 2014

Boeing versus SpaceX

It's always more fun to see a race than one person or one entity. Having Boeing and SpaceX there adds a bit of excitement to things. SpaceX is kind of the up-and-comer. Boeing is the cagey veteran.

—*CNNMoney*, September 18, 2014

Jeff Bezos in Space

Every time I see Jeff Bezos, I say, "Why aren't you doing more in space?"

—SXSW Conference, March 9, 2013

Launch Day

It's pretty nerve-racking, that's for sure. The pucker factor on launch day is very high. . . . I'm actually the chief designer of the rocket. I could redraw that rocket without the benefit of blueprints for the most part, so it's sort of like seeing my baby go up there.

—Inc. 5000 Conference, 2008

Falcon 1

Falcon 1 is just our test vehicle . . . our first foray. It's not the end game. It is the beginning of the beginning.

—Space.com, August 12, 2005

Naming Booster Stages

Why did we name one booster Falcon and one Dragon? Falcon is named after the *Millennium Falcon* from *Star Wars* because Falcon can do the Kessel Run in seven parsecs. And then Dragon was actually named after "Puff, the Magic Dragon" because so many people thought I must be smoking weed to do this venture.

—Google Zeitgeist '08, September 18, 2008

. . . .

Simplicity

It's our mantra because it gets you both reliability and low cost.

—*Discover* magazine, September 8, 2005

. . . .

On Not Reaching Orbit

SpaceX's Falcon 1 failed to reach orbit three times in a row.

Well, we got to space. . . . You don't necessarily go all the way on the first few dates. You've got to work your way up there.

—Inc. 5000 Conference, 2008

We haven't gotten into orbit, true, but we've made considerable progress. If it's an all-or-nothing proposition then we've failed. But it's not all or nothing. We *must* get to orbit eventually, and we will. It might take us one, two or three more tries, but we will. We *will* make it work.

—*Wired*, August 5, 2008

Falcon 1 Flight 4

That was freaking awesome. We made orbit thanks to the hard work of the SpaceX team and all you guys—I mean, that's really what got us to orbit there. There were a lot of people who thought we couldn't do it—a lot, actually—but as the saying goes: fourth time's the charm. This really means a lot to SpaceX, obviously, getting to orbit—that's just a huge milestone. There's only a handful of countries on earth that have done it. It's normally a country thing, not a company thing. So it's just an amazing achievement.

—address to SpaceX employees after Falcon 1 Flight 4,
September 28, 2008

New US Space Strategy

President Obama had just announced a new space strategy, which included terminating the Constellation Program, listing new priorities for NASA, and creating opportunities for private space companies.

I think what this new policy recognizes is that NASA isn't going to get some huge increase in its budget, as occurred in the Apollo era, so if we're to make great progress and make the next giant leaps for mankind, then it has to be done in an affordable manner. And the only way to do that is by harnessing the power of free enterprise, as we use in all other modes of transport.

—*Science Friday*, April 16, 2010

Importance of Pushing Forward

If we don't succeed, then we will be certainly pointed to as a reason why people shouldn't even try for these things. So I think it's important that we do whatever is necessary to keep going.

—International Space Station R&D Conference,
July 7, 2015

First Rocket Landing

The first rocket came in and landed maybe a couple of hundred yards away from the launch site in tiny fragments. That rocket ended up costing around $6 million, compared to other rockets in that class, which were about $25 million.

—Khan Academy Chats, April 17, 2013

RUD

RUD = Rapid Unscheduled Disassembly :)

—Twitter, June 15, 2016

· ·

Reusable Rockets

A fully and rapidly reusable rocket—which has never been done before—is the pivotal breakthrough needed to substantially reduce the cost of space access. While most rockets are designed to burn up on reentry, SpaceX is building rockets that not only withstand reentry, but also land safely on Earth to be refueled and fly again.

—"X Marks the Spot: Falcon 9 Attempts Ocean Platform Landing," December 16, 2014

It's just a very tough engineering problem, and I wasn't sure it could be solved for a while. Relatively recently, in the last 12 months or so, I've come to the conclusion that it can be solved, and SpaceX is going to try to do it. We could fail. I'm not saying we are certain of success here, but we are going to try to do it. We have a design that on paper—doing the calculations, doing the simulations—does work. And now we need to make sure that those simulations and reality agree. Because generally when they don't, reality wins.

—press conference on SpaceX's commitment to develop fully reusable rockets, September 29, 2011

••

The Expense of Expendable Booster Stages

I tell my team, imagine there was a pallet of cash that was plummeting through the atmosphere and it was going to burn up and smash into tiny pieces. Would you try to save it? Probably yes.

—Code Conference, June 1, 2016

••

Reaction to First Vertical Landing

I ran out onto the causeway to watch the landing, and the sonic boom reached me about the same time as the rocket touched down, so I actually thought, at first, that it had exploded. But it turned out to be just that the sonic boom almost exactly coincided with the touchdown point, and the sound reached me several seconds later. I thought, "Well, at least we got close," but then I went back into launch control and it was this amazing video of the rocket still actually standing there on the launchpad, or the landing pad, I should say. I can't quite believe it.

—press teleconference after first vertical landing,
December 21, 2015

I think this is quite significant. I can't say exactly where it would rank, but I do think it's a revolutionary moment. No one has ever brought an orbital-class booster back intact.

—press teleconference after first vertical landing,
December 21, 2015

• •

Reaction to First Vertical Landing at Sea

The Dragon 9 booster had just made history by landing vertically on a SpaceX drone ship in the ocean.

I think this is a really good milestone for the future of spaceflight. It's another step towards the stars. In order for us to really open up access to space, we've got to achieve full and rapid reusability, and being able to do that for the primary rocket booster is going to have a huge impact on cost. It'll still take us a few years to make that smooth and efficient, but I think it's proven that it can work. There probably will be some failures in the future. But we will iron those out and get it to the point where it's routine to bring it back and where the only changes to the rocket are to hose it down, you know, give it a wash, add the propellant, and fly again.

—SpaceX Dragon CRS-8 post-launch news
conference, April 8, 2016

• •

Taking SpaceX Public

SpaceX's objectives are super long-term, and the market is not. I'm a bit worried that if we did go public—certainly if we went public too soon—that that market pressure would force us to do short-term things and abandon long-term projects.

—CHM Revolutionaries, January 22, 2013

Air Force EELV Block Buy

SpaceX filed a bid protest against the Air Force's sole-source Evolved Expendable Launch Vehicle (EELV) contract with United Launch Alliance.

The ULA rockets are about four times more expensive than ours, so this contract is costing the US taxpayers billions of dollars for no reason. And to add salt to the wound, the primary engine used is a Russian-made engine—made in Russia. Moreover, the person who heads up Russian space activities is Dmitryi Rogozin, who is on the sanctions list. So it seems pretty strange. How is it that we're sending hundreds of millions of US taxpayer money at a time when Russia is in the process of invading the Ukraine? It would be hard to imagine some way that Dmitryi Rogozin is not benefiting personally from the dollars that are being sent there. On the surface of it, it appears that there's a good probability of some sanctions violation as well. And we think this deserves to have a spotlight on it. Let's let the sun shine on this. As I say, sunlight is the best disinfectant.

—press conference after Falcon 9's successful
ocean landing, April 14, 2014

• •

Transferring Cargo to and from ISS

NASA has linked us as the primary system for transferring cargo to and from the space station. In fact, our Dragon spacecraft is the only spacecraft capable of taking any significant cargo down from the space station. There are a variety of means of getting to the space station, but in terms of bringing experiments back, which is critical to leverage the value of the space station, our spacecraft is the only one capable of doing that.

—Export-Import Bank Annual Conference,
April 25, 2014

• •

Designing Space Suits

We've actually spent a lot of effort on the space suit design—on both the functionality and the aesthetics. It's actually really hard because if you just optimize for functionality, it's one thing; if you optimize for aesthetics, it doesn't work. Those things that you see in movies, they don't work. So it's like, "How do we make something that looks cool and works?" with the key goal here being that when people see the space suit, we want them to think, "Yeah, I want to wear that thing one day."

—International Space Station R&D Conference,
July 7, 2015

· ·

Dragon V2

Next year, we'll be flying Dragon V2, which is the one that's capable of taking up to seven astronauts to the space station. In fact, Dragon 2 really is a propulsive lander as well, and it's intended to carry astronauts to the space station, but it's also capable of being a general science delivery platform to any-where in the solar system.

—Code Conference, June 1, 2016

· ·

Disagreements with NASA

There were small disagreements here and there . . . like, it seems like the amount of mass and volume reserved for poop is too high. . . . We're like, well, are they really going to do that much poop?

—*GQ*, December 12, 2015

· ·

The Improbable

Certainly, in the beginning, when I told people I was trying to create a rocket company, they thought I was crazy. That seemed like a very improbable thing. And I agreed with them—I think it was im-probable. But sometimes the improbable happens.

—Living Legends of Aviation awards dinner,
January 22, 2010

● ●

A New Frontier

Right now on Earth, you can basically go anywhere in 24 hours. I mean anywhere. You can fly over the Antarctic pole and parachute out 24 hours from now if you want. You can get parachuted to the top of Mount Everest from the right plane. You can go to the bottom of the ocean. [On] Earth, from a physical standpoint, you can go anywhere—anywhere. There is no real physical frontier on Earth anymore, but space is that frontier.

—International Astronautical Congress,
September 27, 2016

ENGINEERING, DESIGN, AND MANUFACTURE

•••

Start in Engineering

My background educationally is physics and economics, and I grew up in sort of an engineering environment—my father is an electromechanical engineer. And so there were lots of enginery things around me. When I asked for an explanation, I got the *true* explanation of how things work. I also did things like make model rockets, and in South Africa there were no premade rockets: I had to go to the chemist and get the ingredients for rocket fuel, mix it, put it in a pipe.

—*Wired*, October 21, 2012

· ·

Favorite Part of the Job

If it was up to me, I would just be doing engineering all day long and designing stuff and testing and trying out different ideas. But I have to do lots of organizational management and finance meetings and talk with investors. What I enjoy the most is just hammering out ideas and trying new things with my engineering team.

—Living Legends of Aviation awards dinner,
January 22, 2010

· ·

Engineering Is Magic

If you go back back a few hundred years, what we take for granted today would seem like magic—being able to talk to people over long distances, to transmit images, flying, accessing vast amounts of data like an oracle. . . . So engineering is, for all intents and purposes, magic, and who wouldn't want to be a magician?

—*Forbes*, March 26, 2012

. . . .

Engineers Should Have Kids

Musk has five sons.

My father was an engineer. . . . If that hadn't been the situation, then I would have had little exposure to it, even in South Africa. Engineers should have more kids—whether it's nature or nurture, [the kids of engineers] are more likely to become engineers. I'm doing my civic duty. I've got to make up for the lost ground of some others.

—Founder Showcase, August 3, 2010

. . . .

Immigration Laws

I think, certainly, we need to take a look at our immigration laws. If there are really talented people doing graduate courses in engineering at our universities, we really don't want to send them home. We want to try to do everything we can to keep them here. For every one person who's an ace engineer, there are probably 10 jobs that will be created if that person stays here. It's a huge multiplier effect.

—Export-Import Bank Annual Conference,
April 25, 2014

• •

Design and Aesthetics

In your brain you have, I think, some intrinsic elements that represent beauty and that trigger the emotion of appreciation for beauty in your mind. And I think that these are actually relatively consistent among people. Not completely—not everyone likes the same thing—but there's a lot of commonality.

—STVP Future Fest, October 7, 2015

• •

Achieving Perfection

Aspirationally, we're in pursuit of the platonic ideal of the perfect car. Who knows what that looks like actually, but you want to try to make every element of the car as flawless as possible. There will always be some degree of imperfection, but we try to minimize that and create a car that is just delightful in every way.

—StartmeupHK Venture Forum, January 26, 2016

• •

Details

You can train yourself to pay attention to the tiny details; I think almost anyone can. This is very much a double-edged sword because then you see all the little details, and then little things drive you crazy.

—STVP Future Fest, October 7, 2015

••

The Challenge of Manufacturing

You can create a demo version of a product, like a few cars' worth of a product, with a small team in maybe three to six months. But to build the machine that builds the machine, it takes at least 100 to 1,000 times more resources and difficulty.

—2016 Tesla Annual Shareholders Meeting,
May 31, 2016

••

Believe in Manufacturing

Tesla believes strongly in making things. They [Google and Apple] do not. That's fine, it's a philosophical difference. We believe that manufacturing technology is itself subject to a tremendous amount of innovation, and in fact, we believe that there's more potential for innovation in manufacturing then there is in the design of a car—by a long shot. This is just a philosophical difference. Perhaps we are wrong. But we believe in manufacturing, and we believe that a company that values manufacturing as highly as we do is going to attract the best minds in manufacturing.

—Tesla Motors Q1 2016 earnings call, May 4, 2016

Model 3 Design

The S was the first car we really designed ourselves, and it was all about just trying to make the car work in the first place. X was basically built off of the S platform but then [it was] even more complicated so, unfortunately, [it was] even harder to make. The Model 3 is the first car Tesla is creating that is designed to be easy to make. This is really a fundamental difference.

—Tesla Motors Q1 2016 earnings call, May 4, 2016

Building the Tesla Factory

We've realized that the true problem, the true difficulty, and where the greatest potential is, is building the machine that makes the machine—in other words, building the factory and really thinking of the factory like a product. . . . We don't try to create a car by ordering a bunch of things off a catalog. We design the car the way it should be and then we, working with suppliers, make all of those individual components. There's almost nothing in a Model S that's in any other car. And I think the same approach is the right approach to take when building the machine maker, the factory. I actually think that the potential for improvement in the machine that makes the machine is a factor of 10 greater than the potential on the car side. I think maybe more than a factor of 10.

—2016 Tesla Annual Shareholders Meeting, May 31, 2016

We're basically going to design a factory like you'd design an advanced computer and, in fact, use engineers that are used to doing that and have them work on this. I've found that once you explain this to a first-rate engineer, the lightbulb goes on. . . . A lot of engineers don't realize that this is possible. They think that there's a wall—they're basically operating according to these invisible walls. So we're in the process of just going through and explaining those walls don't exist.

—2016 Tesla Annual Shareholders Meeting, May 31, 2016

....

Alien Dreadnought

The internal name for designing the machine that makes the machine is the Alien Dreadnought. At the point at which the factory looks like an alien dreadnought, then you know you've won.

—Tesla Motors Q2 2016 earnings call, August 3, 2016

• •

Bidirectional Feedback Loop

I also believe in having a tight feedback loop between engineering and production. If production is far away from engineering, you lose that feedback loop. Someone who designed the car in a particular way doesn't realize that it's very difficult to manufacture in the particular way that it's designed. But if the factory floor is 50 feet away from their desk, then they can go out and they can just see it. It's obvious. And they can have a dialogue with the people on the floor. And likewise, a lot of the people on the manufacturing team have great ideas about how to improve the car, but if they're far away, they can't communicate that to the engineers who designed it. I think that it's something that's often neglected, but having that strong bidirectional feedback loop between engineering and production is really helpful for making the car better, finding efficiencies, and lowering the cost.

—Export-Import Bank Annual Conference,
April 25, 2014

WEALTH AND MONEY

....

Eggs in One Basket

It's OK to have your eggs in one basket as long as you control what happens to that basket. The problem with the Silicon Valley financing model is that you lose control after the first investment round.

—Inc., December 1, 2007

....

Choosing a Venture Capitalist

If you have a choice of a lower valuation with someone you really like or a higher valuation with someone you have a question mark about, take the lower valuation. It's better to have a higher-quality venture capitalist who you think would be great to work with than to get a higher valuation with someone where there's even a question mark, really.

—PandoMonthly, July 12, 2012

••

Investing Your Own Money

My proceeds from PayPal after tax were about $180 million. A hundred of that went into SpaceX, 70 into Tesla, and 10 into SolarCity. And then I literally had to borrow money for rent.

—PandoMonthly, July 12, 2012

I'm a big believer in: don't ask investors to invest their money if you're not prepared to invest your money. I really believe in the opposite philosophy of other people's money. It just doesn't seem right to me that if you ask other people to invest that you shouldn't also invest. . . . I'd rather lose my money than any of my friends' money or investors' money.

—2016 Tesla Annual Shareholders Meeting, May 31, 2016

••

Judging Achievement

The size of the company market cap isn't really a metric by which I would judge my own achievement.

—*Think Tank*, December 13, 2007

∙∙

Giving Away Assets

I was actually at one point of a school of thought that it's best to give away 99 percent or more of one's assets—kind of like the [Warren] Buffett school of thought. I'm still mostly inclined in that direction, but after seeing what happened with Ford, GM, and Chrysler—where GM and Chrysler went bankrupt but Ford did not—Ford seemed to make better long-term choices than the other two companies, in part because of the influence of the Ford family. Then I thought, "OK, there may be some merit in having some longer-term family ownership, at least a portion of it, so it acts as a positive influence."

—CHM Revolutionaries, January 22, 2013

∙∙

Hopes for Children

I certainly hope they will work very hard. I believe they should be productive contributors to society. They shouldn't be trust-fund kids. I'm hopeful they will do things like engineering, or write books, or just, in some way, add more than they take from the world.

—*Telegraph*, August 4, 2007

LIFE LESSONS

••

Enjoy Your Work

There are three things you look for: You have to look forward in the morning to doing your work. You do want to have a significant financial reward. And you want to have a possible effect on the world. If you can find all three, you have something you can tell your children.

—*Pennsylvania Gazette*, November 4, 2008

••

Burning Man Epiphanies

You have to watch those epiphanies at Burning Man. They're not necessarily what you should pursue.

—CHM Revolutionaries, January 22, 2013

••

Turning Possibility into Probability

The first step is to establish that something is possible; then probability will occur.

—*Esquire*, November 14, 2012

• •

Just Be Yourself

Really should be a rule that oatmeal-raisin cookies can't look too much like choc chip. Doppelgänger cookie trickery!

—Twitter, December 20, 2014

Nothing against all the oatmeal-raisin cookies out there. Just be yourself.

—Twitter, December 20, 2014

• •

Long-Term Grudges

Life is too short for long-term grudges.

—*Inc.*, December 1, 2007

• •

Fear

I wouldn't say I'm fearless. In fact, I think I feel fear quite strongly.

—AutoBild.tv, November 6, 2014

Something that can be helpful is fatalism, to some degree. If you just accept the probabilities, then that diminishes fear.

—Y Combinator's "How to Build the Future" series,
September 15, 2016

••

Naysayers

What I find ironic about a lot of the naysayers is that the very same people will transition from saying it was impossible to saying it was obvious. And I'm like, "Wait a second. Was it obvious or impossible? It can't be both."

—Tesla Motors Q1 2016 earnings call, May 4, 2016

••

New York Times Controversy

We assumed that the reporter would be fair and impartial, as has been our experience with the *New York Times*, an organization that prides itself on journalistic integrity. As a result, we did not think to read his past articles and were unaware of his outright disdain for electric cars. We were played for a fool and as a result, let down the cause of electric vehicles. For that, I am deeply sorry.

—"A Most Peculiar Test Drive," February 13, 2013

Critical Reviews

I have no problem with negative feedback, nor do I have a problem with critical reviews. If I had a problem with critical reviews, I would spend all my time battling critical reviews. There have been hundreds of negative articles—hundreds—and yet I've only spoken out a few times. I don't have a problem with critical reviews, I have a problem with false reviews.

—SXSW Conference, March 9, 2013

Physics and the Universe

Interesting to think of physics as a set of compression algorithms for the universe. That's basically what formulas are.

—Twitter, February 16, 2016

· ·

Sleep

I tried to figure out what's the right amount of sleep. I found I could drop below a certain threshold of sleep, and although I'd be awake more hours and I could sustain it, I would get less done because my mental acuity would be affected. So I found, generally, the right number for me is around six to six and a half hours, on average, per night.

—CHM Revolutionaries, January 22, 2013

· ·

Take Risks While Young

As you get older, your obligations increase. And once you have a family, you start taking risks not just for yourself but for your family as well. It gets much harder to do things that might not work out. So now is the time to do that—before you have those obligations. I would encourage you to take risks now; do something bold. You won't regret it.

—commencement address at the University of Southern California, May 16, 2014

. . . .

Waiting for Godot

Have recently come to appreciate the awesome, absurdist humor of *Waiting for Godot*. We so often wait, without knowing why, when or where.

—Twitter, April 17, 2016

. . . .

Work-Life Balance

I always try to reserve time for my kids because I love hanging out with them. Kids are really great. I mean, 99 percent of the time, they make you happier. . . . Of anything in my life, I would say kids by far make me the happiest. A lot of times, kids are kind of in their own worlds. They don't want to talk to their dad for hours on end, generally. So I can be in the same room with them, they can talk to me from time to time, but I can get some e-mails done, get some work done, and then whenever they want to talk to me, they can.

—Code Conference, June 1, 2016

Credit Where It's Due

I just want to emphasize that sometimes—in fact, most of the time—I get way too much credit or attention for what I do. I'm just the visible element. But the reason those companies are successful is because we have extremely talented people at all levels that are making it happen.

—in conversation with Bill Gates, Boao Forum for Asia, March 29, 2015

Trying

If something's important enough, you should try. Even if the probable outcome is failure.

—*60 Minutes*, March 30, 2014

Convincing the Public

If you're trying to convince the public to do something, you have to say, "OK, how's this gonna read? What message are we going to try to convey? What will people respond to? What would I respond to if I was sort of an objective member of the public?" If you're trying to change people's minds or get people fired up about something, then you have to think, "OK, what's that message? What's going to get them really excited?"

—STVP Future Fest, October 7, 2015

• •

Stay Focused

Focus is incredibly important. If you have a certain amount of resources, to the degree that you diffuse your focus, you impede your ability to execute.

—2016 Tesla Annual Shareholders Meeting,
May 31, 2016

• •

Legacy

I think what matters is the actions, not what people think of me in the future. I'll be long dead. But the actions that I take, will they have been useful?

—*GQ*, December 12, 2015

MILESTONES

1971

- Elon Reeve Musk is born in Pretoria, Transvaal, South Africa, to Maye and Errol Musk.

1984

- Musk codes *Blastar*, a BASIC-based video game, and sells it to a computer magazine for $500.

1988

- Musk obtains Canadian citizenship (his mother was born in Canada), moves there, and begins a series of odd jobs.

1990

- Musk begins his undergraduate degree in the Commerce program at Queen's University in Kingston, Ontario. He pays for tuition in part by building custom computers for students.

1992

- After earning a scholarship, Musk transfers to the University of Pennsylvania and begins pursuing dual degrees in economics and physics. He earns money for tuition by hosting large parties with his roommate Adeo Ressi.

1994

- For a school assignment, Musk writes a business plan titled "The Importance of Being Solar," which envisions a solar-powered future.

- Musk completes his degree in economics from the Wharton School of the University of Pennsylvania and decides to stay an extra year to complete his physics degree. (Due to a change in academic requirements, the degrees are not officially issued until 1997.)

1995

- Musk moves to California to study for a PhD in physics and material science at Stanford University but drops out before classes start to cofound Zip2, a software and services provider to the media industry.

1999

- Musk sells Zip2 to Compaq in February for $307 million in cash, which earns Musk $22 million.

- With money from the Zip2 sale, Musk cofounds X.com, an internet finance and money-transfer startup.

2000

- Musk marries Justine Wilson, his college sweetheart, in January.

- X.com merges with Confinity, another internet finance company, which was founded by Peter Thiel, Max Levchin, Luke Nosek, and Ken Howery. Under Musk's direction as CEO, the new X.com focuses its efforts on online payments, the most popular service of both previous companies' offerings. Later in the year, Musk is ousted as CEO.

2001

- X.com is renamed PayPal.

- Musk creates the Musk Foundation, which provides grants to support research and advocacy for renewable energy and human space exploration as well as for pediatric research and science and engineering education.

- Musk devises Mars Oasis, a project that later ignites the public's interest in space—and thereby increases NASA's budget—by proposing to send a miniature greenhouse to Mars to grow plants. During his research, Musk realizes that even with public support, the trip would be too expensive without a breakthrough in rocket technology.

2002

- Musk becomes a citizen of the United States.

- Musk and Justine have their first child, Nevada Alexander, in May. He is named after the state that hosts Burning Man, the annual art and music festival where he was conceived.

- PayPal goes public in February with an IPO of $70 million; Musk is the largest shareholder. Shortly thereafter, eBay acquires PayPal in a deal valued at $1.5 billion, which earns Musk $180 million.

- Ten weeks after his birth, Nevada dies of sudden infant death syndrome.

- After returning from a failed attempt to purchase intercontinental ballistic missiles (ICBMs) in Russia, Musk realizes he can reduce the cost of a rocket (and its launch) by starting a company designing and manufacturing the majority of it in-house.

- With some of the money from the PayPal sale, Musk founds Space Exploration Technologies Corporation (aka SpaceX), hires rocket scientist Tom Mueller, and opens its first headquarters in El Segundo, California.

2003

- Musk has lunch with JB Straubel, during which they discuss their mutual interest in electric vehicles. On Straubel's recommendation, Musk test rides in an electric car prototype called the tzero, developed by AC Propulsion.

- Musk tries to convince AC Propulsion to commercialize the tzero.

2004

- Musk and Straubel team up with Martin Eberhard, Marc Tarpenning, and Ian Wright, who had already incorporated a company called Tesla Motors, to commercialize the tzero electric sports car concept. Musk invests $6.5 million in the new company, leading the Series A funding round. He becomes chairman of the board and takes an active role in designing the new car, called the Tesla Roadster.

- Elon and Justine have twins, whom they name Griffin and Xavier.

2005

- Tesla makes its first successful Roadster test mule using a modified Lotus Elise chassis, the Tesla battery pack, and the AC Propulsion drivetrain.

- Musk and Valor Equity Partners lead Tesla's $13 million Series B funding round.

- The US Air Force awards SpaceX an indefinite delivery/indefinite quantity (IDIQ) contract for Responsive Small Spacelift (RSS) launches.

- SpaceX announces plans to develop Falcon 9, a heavy-lift launch vehicle.

- Musk makes a cameo in *Thank You for Smoking*, a film that he executive produced.

2006

- Falcon 1, the third orbital launch vehicle in history to be developed by private funds, fails its first launch.

- Musk coleads Tesla's $40 million Series C funding round, which also receives investments from Sergey Brin and Larry Page.

- Musk helps his cousins Peter and Lyndon Rive create SolarCity and serves as company chair.

- Tesla completes the Roadster prototype with Musk serving as chief designer. It is unveiled to the public, and Tesla starts taking reservations. Within two weeks, 127 reservations are taken.

- In August, SpaceX earns a $278 million NASA contract under the Commercial Orbital Transportation Services (COTS) program to develop the ability to carry and return cargo from the International Space Station (ISS). This helps fund the development of Falcon 9, the Dragon capsule, and vehicle test flights.

- Musk and Justine have triplets, whom they name Damian, Saxon, and Kai.

- Mikhail Gorbachev presents Musk with a Global Green Product/Industrial Design Award for the Tesla Roadster.

2007

- Tesla faces numerous struggles while trying to reach the Roadster delivery date, including the need to replace the drive units in all Roadster version 1 vehicles and to completely redesign the motor.

- Falcon 1 fails to reach orbit on its second launch.

- Tesla's fourth round of financing earns $45 million, which bring the total amount of private financing to $105.5 million.

- Eberhard steps down (or is ousted, depending on who you talk to) as Tesla CEO and is temporally replaced by Michael Marks, which leads to several lawsuits between Eberhard and Musk. Ze'ev Drori steps in as CEO.

- *Inc.* magazine names Musk Entrepreneur of the Year.

- *R&D* magazine names Musk Innovator of the Year.

- Tesla wins an INDEX: Award for the Tesla Roadster design.

2008

- Tesla moves its battery pack factory from Thailand to the Bay Area—which is highly unusual in traditional manufacturing—in order to tighten its supply chain. This decision paves the way for Tesla's trademark vertical integration manufacturing methods.

- The first Tesla Roadster, a luxury sports car, is delivered to a customer (Musk himself), and it essentially does not work.

- Tesla begins the process of completely rebooting the Roadster's design, technology, and manufacture, as well as replacing most of its suppliers. The company is in grave financial trouble. However, Roadster is in regular production by March, making it the only zero-emissions car in production.

- Tesla's first retail store opens in Los Angeles on Santa Monica Boulevard with a focus on improving the traditional car-buying experience.

- NASA awards SpaceX a Launch Services IDIQ contract for Falcon 1 and Falcon 9 launches.

- Tesla announces Model S, a sedan that is projected to cost about $50,000.

- In August, Falcon 1 fails to reach orbit a third time.

- Tesla hires Franz von Holzhausen as its chief designer.

- Falcon 1 reaches orbit in September, making it the first privately funded, liquid-fuel rocket to do so. Significantly, this was the last launch Musk could afford to fund.

- Musk and Justine file for divorce. Soon after the filing, Musk starts dating British actress Talulah Riley, whom he meets at a club in London.

- Musk takes over as Tesla CEO in October; layoffs commence.

- Musk wins the American Institute of Aeronautics and Astronautics George M. Low Space Transportation Award for his Falcon 1 design and is named one of *Esquire*'s 75 most influential people of the 21st century.

- In the midst of the national financial crisis, SpaceX's Falcon 9 and Dragon capsule win a $1.6 billion, 12-mission commercial resupply services (CRS) contract from NASA. These missions are to occur only after the COTS missions are deemed successful. This contract, along with a last-minute financing round of $40 million, helps SpaceX narrowly avoid bankruptcy.

2009

- Tesla auditions two electric car prototypes for Daimler, which leads to Tesla's first powertrain development contract, an ongoing partnership with Daimler, and a $50 million investment. These developments put the struggling Tesla on firmer ground financially and give it credibility in the auto community.

- Tesla recalls 75 percent of Roadsters that have been produced since March 2008.

- The US Department of Energy (DOE) approves Tesla for a $465 million loan under the Advanced Technology Vehicles Manufacturing (ATVM) loan program.

- On its fifth flight, Falcon 1 delivers the RazakSAT satellite, its first commercial payload, into orbit in July. The rocket is subsequently retired and replaced by Falcon 9.

- Musk receives an Aviation Week Laureate Award for his contributions to the space industry, earns the National Space Society's Wernher von Braun Memorial Award, which is presented to important leaders in the space industry.

2010

- Tesla receives $465 million in funding from the DOE loan.

- Toyota invests $50 million in Tesla, and the two companies partner to develop technologies. As part of the deal, Tesla purchases part of Toyota and GM's NUMMI automotive plant in Fremont, California. Tesla formally takes over the entire plant and officially opens the Tesla factory later in the year.

- Tesla goes public with an IPO valued at $226.1 million, making it the first US car company since Ford to go public.

- Falcon 9 launches successfully on its first flight in June. In the same month, Iridium Communications awards SpaceX the largest commercial space contract in history, worth $492 million.

- Musk marries Talulah Riley in September.

- Musk makes a cameo in *Iron Man 2*.

- The Musk Foundation and SolarCity donate a solar-power system to the South Bay Communities Alliance's (SBCA) Hurricane Response Center in Coden, Alabama.

- *Time* magazine names Musk one of the most influential people in the world. He is also named the worldwide Automotive Executive of the Year, making him the youngest person to earn the title.

- The Fédération Aéronautique Internationale (FAI), the world's governing body for air sports, presents Musk with a Gold Space Medal for Falcon 1.

- During the COTS Demo Flight 1 mission in December (Falcon 9's second launch), SpaceX launches, orbits, and recovers the Dragon spacecraft, becoming the first private company to do so.

2011

- Tesla unveils the Model S Beta prototype to the public.

- New milestones are added to SpaceX's original NASA COTS contract, bringing the total value up to $396 million.

- SpaceX releases development costs for Falcon 9 v1.0: just over $300 million. This is about $3.6 billion less than NASA estimates costs would have been if a traditional cost-plus contract had been used.

- *Forbes* names Musk one of America's 20 Most Powerful CEOs 40 and Under, and *WSJ. Magazine* names him Innovator of the Year in Technology.

- Musk wins the Heinlein Prize for Advances in Space Commercialization.

2012

- Private markets estimate SpaceX's value around $1.3 billion in February.

- Tesla unveils Model X, a full-sized luxury crossover SUV.

- In May, during its first commercial resupply mission, the Dragon spacecraft becomes the first privately developed vehicle to berth with the ISS. After this flight, private markets estimate SpaceX's valuation at $2.4 billion, nearly double what it was at the beginning of the year.

- Tesla starts delivering Model S, the first premium electric sedan, to customers.

- The Massachusetts State Automobile Dealers Association sues Tesla, alleging that state franchise law forbids Tesla from selling directly to consumers. In the years to come, other dealership organizations will follow similar paths in an effort to ban Tesla from selling cars in their states.

- SpaceX is contracted to launch the National Oceanic and Atmospheric Administration's Jason-3 spacecraft, the company's first science mission for NASA Launch Services.

- SpaceX signs a $440 million contract with NASA to develop a new crew-carrying space capsule by 2017.

- For the first time, SpaceX's Grasshopper—a vertical takeoff, vertical landing test vehicle—"hops" six feet in the air, the first step toward making Falcon 9's first stage fully and rapidly reusable.

- Tesla unveils the first six secretly constructed stations of the Supercharger network, which allows Tesla owners to travel long distances and recharge, free of cost.

- Musk and Talulah Riley file for divorce.

- In December, the US Air Force Space and Missile Systems Center contracts SpaceX for two Evolved Expendable Launch Vehicle (EELV) missions.

- Model S is named the 2013 Motor Trend Car of the Year, and it wins *Automobile* magazine's Automobile of the Year award.

- *Smithsonian* magazine awards Musk the American Ingenuity Award for technology, and Musk earns a spot on *Forbes*'s The World's Billionaires list. Additionally, the Royal Aeronautical Society presents Musk with the Gold Medal, its highest honor.

- SpaceX has more than 40 launches on its manifest by year's end.

2013

- A Massachusetts Superior Court judge dismisses the lawsuit brought against Tesla by car dealerships claiming the Tesla sales model violates state franchise regulations. Later in the year, a New York Supreme Court judge makes a similar ruling for a lawsuit in his state.

- SpaceX completes the fifth consecutive successful launch of its Falcon 9 rocket and Dragon spacecraft.

- In May, Tesla repays its DOE loan in full nine years early, making it the only American car company to ever have paid back the government in full.

- In July, Musk and Talulah Riley remarry.

- Model S earns a five-star safety rating from the US National Highway Traffic Safety Administration and sets a new safety record for the lowest likelihood of injury to occupants.

- Tesla opens a new assembly plant in the Netherlands and announces a European Supercharger network.

- Musk posts a 58-page paper on the Hyperloop, his open-source concept for a fifth mode of transportation.

- Grasshopper, the Falcon 9 test rig, demonstrates its ability to fly, steer, and land in a 100-meter "lateral divert test."

- Falcon 9 v1.1, the second version of Falcon 9, makes its first flight during a demo mission to launch Canada's CASSIOPE satellite.

- In its final flight, Grasshopper rises to an altitude of 744 meters—its highest leap ever—before hovering and descending safely to its launchpad. SpaceX retires the vehicle after the flight.

- SpaceX successfully delivers the SES-8 satellite into orbit, making it the first private company to send a satellite into geosynchronous transfer orbit.

- *Fortune* magazine names Musk its Businessperson of the Year.

- SpaceX has almost 50 launches on its manifest by year's end, and Tesla has made more than 20,000 cars, a huge increase from the number of cars manufactured in previous years.

2014

- The Falcon 9 booster soft-lands in the Atlantic Ocean, making it the first successful controlled ocean touchdown of a liquid-rocket-engine orbital booster.

- SpaceX files a protest in the US Court of Federal Claims to challenge the US Air Force's EELV contract with United Launch Alliance (ULA) (the space technology partnership between Boeing and Lockheed Martin), claiming that the launches in question should be opened up to competition from other providers. Musk later testifies against ULA at the US Senate Hearing on National Security Space Launch Programs.

- SpaceX unveils Dragon V2, which is a spacecraft designed to carry astronauts to and from destinations in space.

- Tesla announces it will open its patents for others' use and that it will not pursue patent-related lawsuits.

- For the first time, Tesla's Supercharger network delivers more than 1 GWh of energy to Model S vehicles in a single month (June).

- Tesla announces plans to construct the Gigafactory in partnership with Panasonic. The factory will be designed to produce battery cells at scale, thus reducing their cost.

- Musk agrees to donate $1 million to the construction of the Tesla Science Center at Wardenclyffe, a project of cartoonist Matthew Inman.

- SpaceX wins $2.6 billion of a $6.8 billion NASA contract to ferry astronauts to the ISS under the Commercial Crew Program (CCP), which was expected to go entirely to Boeing.

- Tesla announces dual motor, all-wheel drive, and auto-pilot capabilities for Model S.

- The Tesla fleet's cumulative worldwide miles surpass half a billion.

- SpaceX completes the manufacture of the 100th Merlin 1D engine, which it uses to power Falcon 9.

- In December, Musk files for a second divorce from Talulah Riley but later withdraws the motion.

2015

- Musk donates $10 million to the Future of Life Institute to fund research focused on keeping artificial intelligence beneficial.

- In January, Falcon 9 successfully launches the Dragon spacecraft and attempts to land at sea on the *Just Read the Instructions* drone ship. It comes in too fast and explodes. In April, Falcon 9 successfully launches another Dragon spacecraft and attempts the same landing, failing again.

- SpaceX and the US Air Force reach a settlement agreement regarding the EELV program.

- SpaceX completes a $1 billion financing round, which includes two new investors: Google and Fidelity.

- SpaceX successfully launches two satellites at once, a technique that has never been attempted before. Per satellite, the mission costs less than $30 million.

- Tesla unveils the Powerwall and Powerpack, stationary energy-storage solutions for residential and commercial use, respectively.

- In May, Falcon 9 is certified for national security space missions, which means it can bid against ULA for EELV contracts.

- SpaceX's Crew Dragon, a vehicle designed to carry astronauts, successfully demonstrates its abort system as part of its ongoing developments for NASA's Commercial Crew Program.

- The Tesla fleet logs its billionth mile driven in June.

- SpaceX asks the federal government for permission to pursue an internet satellite network, a project that would provide satellite internet to remote parts of the world.

- SpaceX announces a Hyperloop pod competition for college students and independent engineering groups, as well as plans to build a Hyperloop test track where teams can test their human-scale pods.

- Tesla begins delivering the first Model X vehicles.

- Musk announces OpenAI, a nonprofit organization dedicated to democratizing artificial intelligence and keeping it beneficial and safe for the future.

- Falcon 9 Full Thrust, the third version of Falcon 9 and the first to include a "reusable" first stage, has its maiden flight. It delivers 11 satellites into orbit, returns to Earth, and lands vertically at Kennedy Space Center, making it the first orbital rocket first stage to do so. This achievement is a significant step toward SpaceX's goal of rocket reusability.

- *Forbes* names Musk No. 38 on The World's Most Powerful People list and No. 34 on the Forbes 400.

2016

- Tesla releases version 7.1 beta software for its Model S and Model X, which includes the Summon and Autopark features.

- Tesla unveils Model 3, the most affordable mass-market electric vehicle. Within a week, more than 300,000 reservations are placed. Production is scheduled to launch by the end of 2017.

- In March, Talulah Riley files for divorce, and it's announced that this time, the action will proceed.

- Falcon 9 rocket successfully launches the Dragon capsule to deliver ISS supplies, returns to Earth, and lands vertically at sea on the *Of Course I Still Love You* drone ship. This is the first water landing of a first stage orbital capable rocket. This feat was repeated on May 6, May 27, and August 14.

- The US Air Force awards SpaceX an $82.7 million contract to launch a new GPS satellite on Falcon 9 in May 2018, effectively breaking the decade-long monopoly Boeing and Lockheed Martin has had on US military launches.

- As part of a private-public partnership with NASA, SpaceX announces plans to launch a modified Dragon capsule lander to Mars as early as 2018.

- Tesla opens the Gigafatory, the world's largest battery factory.

- Tesla bids to acquire SolarCity for $2.6 billion, which would make Tesla the only vertically integrated sustainable energy company in the world. Despite much critical speculation from outsiders, 85 percent of Tesla shareholders unaffiliated with SolarCity voted to approve the deal.

- Musk publishes "Master Plan, Part Deux," in which he announces plans to unveil the electric Tesla Semi and electric public transportation vehicles in 2017.

- Tesla announces a 100 kWh battery pack for its Model S and Model X vehicles, which allows 315 miles and 289 miles, respectively, on a single charge. This upgraded pack also makes Model S the fastest production car in the world, as it can accelerate from 0 to 60 miles per hour in 2.5 seconds.

- Falcon 9 explodes on the launchpad at Kennedy Space Center during a routine propellant fill operation, destroying the rocket and its satellite payload.

- The *Drive* names Musk No. 1 on its list of The 10 Most Influential People in the Business of Cars and No. 2 on its list of The 10 Most Influential People in Automotive Technology. Musk is also named one of *Forbes*'s Global Game Changers and ranks No. 15 on *Forbes*'s The Richest People in Tech list.

- SpaceX's first launch using a reused rocket is scheduled for the fourth quarter of 2016.

CITATIONS

EARLY YEARS

Growing Up in South Africa

Musk, Elon. "10 Questions for Elon Musk." *Time*. July 19, 2010. http://content.time.com/time/magazine /article/0,9171,2002512,00.html.

Daum, Meghan. "Elon Musk Wants to Change How (and Where) Humans Live." *Vogue*. September 21, 2015. http://www.vogue.com/13349221/elon-musk-profile -entrepreneur-spacex-tesla-motors/.

The Hitchhiker's Guide to the Galaxy

Musk, Elon. Interview with Alison van Diggelen. Computer History Museum Revolutionaries, Mountain View, CA. January 22, 2013. https://www.youtube.com/watch?v =AHHwXUm3iIg.

Vance, Ashlee. "Elon Musk, the 21st Century Industrialist." *Bloomberg*. September 14, 2012. http://www.bloomberg .com/news/articles/2012-09-13/elon-musk-the-21st -century-industrialist.

Why Silicon Valley?

Musk, Elon. Interview with Alison van Diggelen. Computer History Museum Revolutionaries, Mountain View, CA. January 22, 2013. https://www.youtube.com/watch?v =AHHwXUm3iI.

Education

Musk, Elon. Interview with Alison van Diggelen. Computer History Museum Revolutionaries, Mountain View, CA. January 22, 2013. https://www.youtube.com/watch?v =AHHwXUm3iI.

College Dating

Musk, Elon. Interview with Alison van Diggelen. Computer History Museum Revolutionaries, Mountain View, CA. January 22, 2013. https://www.youtube.com/watch?v=AHHwXUm3iI.

Choosing a Career Path

Musk, Elon. Interview with Steve Jurvetson. Stanford Technology Ventures Program Future Fest, Stanford University, Stanford, CA. October 7, 2015. https://www.youtube.com/watch?v=Zos-y4VJsdk.

Starting an Internet Company

Musk, Elon. Interview with Hu Shuli. *Who's Time*. Caixin Media. April 22, 2014. https://www.youtube.com/watch?v=XTWTAUBmc6k.

Musk, Elon. Interview with Steve Jurvetson. Stanford Technology Ventures Program Future Fest, Stanford University, Stanford, CA. October 7, 2015. https://www.youtube.com/watch?v=Zos-y4VJsdk.

1995 Funding Climate

Musk, Elon. Interview with John Battelle. Web 2.0 Summit, San Francisco, CA. November 7, 2008. https://www.youtube.com/watch?v=bdCXcu3juhE.

Zip2

Musk, Elon. Lecture at Stanford University. Stanford, CA. October 8, 2003. https://youtu.be/afZTrfvB2AQ.

X.com

Musk, Elon. Interview with Alison van Diggelen. Computer History Museum Revolutionaries, Mountain View, CA. January 22, 2013. https://www.youtube.com/watch?v=AHHwXUm3iI.

PayPal Beginnings

Musk, Elon. Interview with Sarah Lacy. PandoMonthly: Fireside Chat with Elon Musk, Santa Monica, CA. July 12, 2012. https://www.youtube.com/watch?v=uegOUmgKB4E.

LEARNING AND LOGIC

Best Teacher

Musk, Elon. "I Am Elon Musk, CEO/CTO of a Rocket
Company, AMA!" Reddit. January 6, 2015. https://www
.reddit.com/r/IAmA/comments/2rgsan/i_am_elon_musk
_ceocto_of_a_rocket_company_ama.

Critical Thinking

Musk, Elon. "IPO Spotlight with Elon Musk." CLEAN-tech
Investor Summit, Palm Springs, CA. January 19, 2011.
https://www.youtube.com/watch?v=lN6T4ATfgeA.

First Principles Thinking

Musk, Elon. "Elon Musk: The Mind Behind Tesla, SpaceX,
SolarCity. . . ." TED Talk, Long Beach, CA. February 27,
2013. https://www.ted.com/talks/elon_musk_the_mind
_behind_tesla_spacex_solarcity.

Explaining the "Why"

Musk, Elon. Interview with Sal Khan. Khan Academy
Chats, Mountain View, CA. April 17, 2013. https://www
.khanacademy.org/talks-and-interviews/khan-academy
-living-room-chats/v/elon-musk.

How to Learn

Musk, Elon. "I Am Elon Musk, CEO/CTO of a Rocket
Company, AMA!" Reddit. January 6, 2015. https://www
.reddit.com/r/IAmA/comments/2rgsan/i_am_elon_musk
_ceocto_of_a_rocket_company_ama.

Learning Something New

Anderson, Chris. "Elon Musk's Mission to Mars." *Wired*.
October 21, 2012. http://www.wired.com/2012/10/ff-elon
-musk-qa/.

Musk, Elon. Conversation with Bill Gates. Boao Forum for
Asia, Boao, China. March 29, 2015. https://www.youtube
.com/watch?v=TRpjhIhpuiU.

Necessity of a University Degree

Musk, Elon. Interview with Chris Anderson. South by Southwest Conference, Austin, TX. March 9, 2013. https://www.youtube.com/watch?v=LeQMWdOMa-A.

Dedication to Learning

Musk, Elon. Lecture at Stanford University. Stanford, CA. October 8, 2003. https://youtu.be/afZTrfvB2AQ.

Structured Learning

Musk, Elon. Interview with Chris Anderson. South by Southwest Conference, Austin, TX. March 9, 2013. https://www.youtube.com/watch?v=LeQMWdOMa-A.

Inventing Solutions

Musk, Elon. Interview with David Kestenbaum. *Morning Edition*. NPR. August 9, 2007. https://www.youtube.com/watch?v=3dX-Z9p7sQM.

The Truth

Musk, Elon. "Elon Musk Gets Introspective." AutoBild.tv. November 6, 2014. https://www.youtube.com/watch?v=IooquUJmM9M.

BUSINESS

Starting a Business Is Not Fun

Musk, Elon. Interview with Sal Khan. Khan Academy Chats, Mountain View, CA. April 17, 2013. https://www.khanacademy.org/talks-and-interviews/khan-academy-living-room-chats/v/elon-musk.

Usefulness over Money

Musk, Elon. Conversation with Bill Gates. Boao Forum for Asia, Boao, China. March 29, 2015. https://www.youtube.com/watch?v=TRpjhIhpuiU.

Profit as Motive

Musk, Elon. Interview with Sal Khan. Khan Academy Chats, Mountain View, CA. April 17, 2013. https://www.khanacademy.org/talks-and-interviews/khan-academy-living-room-chats/v/elon-musk.

The Purpose of a Company

Musk, Elon. "Elon Musk Gets Introspective." AutoBild.tv. November 6, 2014. https://www.youtube.com/watch?v=IooquUJmM9M.

Compelling Product, Compelling Price

Musk, Elon. Interview with Max Chafkin. Inc. 5000 Conference, National Harbor, MD. 2008. https://www.youtube.com/watch?v=Xcut1JfTMoM.

40 Hours a Week

Daum, Meghan. "Elon Musk Wants to Change How (and Where) Humans Live." *Vogue*. September 21, 2015. http://www.vogue.com/13349221/elon-musk-profile-entrepreneur-spacex-tesla-motors/.

Creating a Productive Environment

Musk, Elon. Address at 2016 Tesla Annual Shareholders Meeting, Mountain View, CA. May 31, 2016. https://www.youtube.com/watch?v=DvVlNkL8f_0.

Staffing

Reingold, Jennifer. "Hondas in Space." *Fast Company*. February 1, 2005. http://www.fastcompany.com/52065/hondas-space.

Interviewing Candidates

Musk, Elon. "Elon Musk Gets Introspective." AutoBild.tv. November 6, 2014. https://www.youtube.com/watch?v=IooquUJmM9M.

A Good Heart Matters

Musk, Elon. Interview with Chris Anderson. South by
Southwest Conference, Austin, TX. March 9, 2013.
https://www.youtube.com/watch?v=LeQMWdOMa-A.

"Special Forces" Approach to Firing

Musk, Elon. Interview with John Battelle. Web 2.0 Summit,
San Francisco, CA. November 7, 2008. https://www
.youtube.com/watch?v=bdCXcu3juhE.

Choosing a CEO

Musk, Elon. "Elon Musk Gets Introspective." AutoBild.tv.
November 6, 2014. https://www.youtube.com/watch?v
=IooquUJmM9M.

CEOs and Their Technology

Hoffman, Carl. "Elon Musk, the Rocket Man with a Sweet
Ride." *Smithsonian* magazine. December 2012. http://www
.smithsonianmag.com/science-nature/elon-musk-the
-rocket-man-with-a-sweet-ride-136059680/?no-ist.

Are You a Good Boss?

Musk, Elon. Interview with Jason Stein. Automotive News
World Congress, Detroit, MI. January 13, 2015.
https://www.youtube.com/watch?v=TK90S7HS3Ng.

Competitors

Musk, Elon. Interview with Kristie Lu Stout. StartmeupHK
Venture Forum, Hong Kong. January 26, 2016.
https://www.youtube.com/watch?v=jiRLGpm5CiY.

Encouraging Innovation

Musk, Elon. Interview at Offshore Northern Seas, Stavanger,
Norway. August 2014. https://www.youtube.com/watch?v
=oZsVxSDB7NY.
Musk, Elon. Conversation with Bill Gates. Boao Forum for
Asia, Boao, China. March 29, 2015. https://www.youtube
.com/watch?v=TRpjhIhpuiU.

Interns

Musk, Elon. Address at 2016 Tesla Annual Shareholders
Meeting, Mountain View, CA. May 31, 2016. https://www
.youtube.com/watch?v=DvVlNkL8f_0.

MBAs at SpaceX

Musk, Elon. Interview with Jaime Peraire. Massachusetts
Institute of Technology Aeronautics and Astronautics
Centennial Symposium, Cambridge, MA. October 24, 2014.
https://www.youtube.com/watch?v=PULkWGHeIQQ.

The Problem with Professional Managers

Chafkin, Max. "Entrepreneur of the Year, 2007: Elon Musk."
Inc. December 1, 2007. http://www.inc.com/magazine
/20071201/entrepreneur-of-the-year-elon-musk.html.

Pitfalls of "Process"

Anderson, Chris. "Elon Musk's Mission to Mars." *Wired*.
October 21, 2012. http://www.wired.com/2012/10/ff-elon
-musk-qa/.

Skip-Level Meetings

Musk, Elon. Interview with Ted Craver. Edison Electric
Institute Annual Convention, New Orleans, LA. June 8,
2015. https://www.youtube.com/watch?v=5nMcJxA3lto.

Meetings Philosophy

Musk, Elon. Interview with Ted Craver. Edison Electric
Institute Annual Convention, New Orleans, LA. June 8,
2015. https://www.youtube.com/watch?v=5nMcJxA3lto.

Soliciting Feedback

Musk, Elon. Interview with Chris Anderson. South by
Southwest Conference, Austin, TX. March 9, 2013.
https://www.youtube.com/watch?v=LeQMWdOMa-A.

Why Companies Fail

Heath, Chris. "How Elon Musk Plans on Reinventing the
World (and Mars)." *GQ*. December 12, 2015. http://www
.gq.com/story/elon-musk-mars-spacex-tesla-interview.

Coming Close to Failure

Musk, Elon. Interview with Hu Shuli. *Who's Time*. Caixin Media. April 22, 2014. https://www.youtube.com/watch?v=XTWTAUBmc6k.

Musk, Elon. Interview with Steve Jurvetson. Stanford Technology Ventures Program Future Fest, Stanford University, Stanford, CA. October 7, 2015. https://www.youtube.com/watch?v=Zos-y4VJsdk.

Failure in Silicon Valley

Musk, Elon. Interview with Steve Jurvetson. Stanford Technology Ventures Program Future Fest, Stanford University, Stanford, CA. October 7, 2015. https://www.youtube.com/watch?v=Zos-y4VJsdk.

Keys to Success

Musk, Elon. Interview with Andrew Ross Sorkin. Vanity Fair New Establishment Summit, San Francisco, CA. October 2015. https://www.youtube.com/watch?v=SqE0107j-uw.

INNOVATION, TECHNOLOGY, AND THOUGHTS ABOUT THE FUTURE

Let Innovation Evolve

Musk, Elon. Conversation with Bill Gates. Boao Forum for Asia, Boao, China. March 29, 2015. https://www.youtube.com/watch?v=TRpjhIhpuiU.

Importance of New Entrants

Musk, Elon. Interview with Sarah Lacy. PandoMonthly: Fireside Chat with Elon Musk, Santa Monica, CA. July 12, 2012. https://www.youtube.com/watch?v=uegOUmgKB4E.

State of Innovation Today

Musk, Elon. Interview with Kara Swisher and Walt Mossberg. Code Conference 2016, Rancho Palos Verdes, CA. June 1, 2016. https://www.youtube.com/watch?v=wsixsRI-Sz4.

Government and Innovation

Musk, Elon. Interview with Alison van Diggelen. Computer History Museum Revolutionaries, Mountain View, CA. January 22, 2013. https://www.youtube.com/watch?v=AHHwXUm3iI.

Disruptive Change

Musk, Elon. Interview with Chris Anderson. South by Southwest Conference, Austin, TX. March 9, 2013. https://www.youtube.com/watch?v=LeQMWdOMa-A.

Be Useful

Musk, Elon. Interview with Steve Jurvetson. Stanford Technology Ventures Program Future Fest, Stanford University, Stanford, CA. October 7, 2015. https://www.youtube.com/watch?v=Zos-y4VJsdk.

Musk, Elon. Interview with Sam Altman. Y Combinator's "How to Build the Future" series, Fremont, CA. September 15, 2016. https://www.youtube.com/watch?v=tnBQmEqBCYo.

Internet

Musk, Elon. Interview with Steve Jurvetson. Stanford Technology Ventures Program Future Fest, Stanford University, Stanford, CA. October 7, 2015. https://www.youtube.com/watch?v=Zos-y4VJsdk.

AI Acceleration

Musk, Elon. Interview with Steve Jurvetson. Stanford Technology Ventures Program Future Fest, Stanford University, Stanford, CA. October 7, 2015. https://www.youtube.com/watch?v=Zos-y4VJsdk.

OpenAI

Musk, Elon. Interview with Sam Altman. Y Combinator's "How to Build the Future" series, Fremont, CA. September 15, 2016. https://www.youtube.com/watch?v=tnBQmEqBCYo.

Musk, Elon. Interview with Kara Swisher and Walt Mossberg. Code Conference 2016, Rancho Palos Verdes, CA. June 1, 2016. https://www.youtube.com/watch?v=wsixsRI-Sz4.

Neural Lace

Musk, Elon. Interview with Kara Swisher and Walt Mossberg. Code Conference 2016, Rancho Palos Verdes, CA. June 1, 2016. https://www.youtube.com/watch?v=wsixsRI-Sz4.
Musk, Elon. Twitter post. June 4, 2016, 1:08 a.m. https://twitter.com/elonmusk/status/739006012749799424.

Being a Cyborg

Musk, Elon. Interview with Kara Swisher and Walt Mossberg. Code Conference 2016, Rancho Palos Verdes, CA. June 1, 2016. https://www.youtube.com/watch?v=wsixsRI-Sz4.

Electric Transport

Musk, Elon. "Elon Musk: The Mind Behind Tesla, SpaceX, SolarCity. . . ." TED Talk, Long Beach, CA. February 27, 2013. https://www.ted.com/talks/elon_musk_the_mind_behind_tesla_spacex_solarcity.

Improving Battery Technology

Musk, Elon. Interview with Margaret Leinen. American Geophysical Union Fall Meeting Presidential Forum, San Francisco, CA. December 15, 2015. https://www.youtube.com/watch?v=b2LCK9dw9as.
Musk, Elon. Tesla Motors Q3 2014 earnings call. November 5, 2014. https://www.youtube.com/watch?v=TzquCoUSTEA.

Autonomous Driving

Heath, Chris. "How Elon Musk Plans on Reinventing the World (and Mars)." *GQ*. December 12, 2015. http://www.gq.com/story/elon-musk-mars-spacex-tesla-interview.
Cellan-Jones, Rory. "Tesla Chief Elon Musk Says Apple Is Making an Electric Car." BBC. January 11, 2016. http://www.bbc.com/news/technology-35280633.

Supersonic Electric Jet

Musk, Elon. Video at Living Legends of Aviation awards dinner, Beverly Hills, CA. January 22, 2010. https://www.youtube.com/watch?v=QXH-puBE1oQ.

Flying Cars

Musk, Elon. Interview with Kristie Lu Stout. StartmeupHK Venture Forum, Hong Kong. January 26, 2016. https://www.youtube.com/watch?v=jiRLGpm5CiY.

Hyperloop

Musk, Elon. Interview with Sarah Lacy. PandoMonthly: Fireside Chat with Elon Musk, Santa Monica, CA. July 12, 2012. https://www.youtube.com/watch?v=uegOUmgKB4E.

Musk, Elon. Interview with Kara Swisher and Walt Mossberg. Code Conference 2016, Rancho Palos Verdes, CA. June 1, 2016. https://www.youtube.com/watch?v=wsixsRI-Sz4.

Tunnels

Musk, Elon. Interview with Kristie Lu Stout. StartmeupHK Venture Forum, Hong Kong. January 26, 2016. https://www.youtube.com/watch?v=jiRLGpm5CiY.

Bogus Space Ventures

Musk, Elon. Lecture at Stanford University. Stanford, CA. October 8, 2003. https://www.youtube.com/watch?v=afZTrfvB2AQ.

Space Entrepreneurs

Musk, Elon. Interview with Michael Suffredini. International Space Station Research and Development Conference, Boston, MA. July 7, 2015. https://www.youtube.com/watch?v=hJD0MMP4nkM.

Orbital Synchronization

Daum, Meghan. "Elon Musk Wants to Change How (and Where) Humans Live." *Vogue.* September 21, 2015. http://www.vogue.com/13349221/elon-musk-profile-entrepreneur-spacex-tesla-motors/.

Price of Interplanetary Humanity

Musk, Elon. Presentation at the International Astronautical Congress, Guadalajara, Mexico. September 27, 2016. https://www.youtube.com/watch?v=10gECHeMSds.

Simulated Reality

Musk, Elon. Twitter post. August 3, 2014, 12:18 p.m. https://twitter.com/elonmusk/status/496012177103663104.

Loss of Technology

Musk, Elon. Presentation at the International Astronautical Congress, Guadalajara, Mexico. September 27, 2016. https://www.youtube.com/watch?v=10gECHeMSds.

TESLA

Master Plan

Musk, Elon. "The Secret Tesla Motors Master Plan (Just between You and Me)." Tesla.com (blog). August 2, 2006. https://www.Tesla.com/blog/secret-tesla-motors-master -plan-just-between-you-and-me.

Genesis of Tesla

Musk, Elon. Interview with Alison van Diggelen. Computer History Museum Revolutionaries, Mountain View, CA. January 22, 2013. https://www.youtube.com/watch?v =AHHwXUm3iI.

Money Is Not Motivation

Musk, Elon. Interview with Sal Khan. Khan Academy Chats, Mountain View, CA. April 17, 2013. https://www .khanacademy.org/talks-and-interviews/khan-academy -living-room-chats/v/elon-musk.

Musk, Elon. Interview with Jason Stein. Automotive News World Congress, Detroit, MI. January 13, 2015. https://www.youtube.com/watch?v=TK90S7HS3Ng.

Musk, Elon. Address at 2016 Tesla Annual Shareholders
Meeting, Mountain View, CA. May 31, 2016. https://www
.youtube.com/watch?v=DvVlNkL8f_0.

Mistakes

Musk, Elon. Interview with Ron Baron. Baron Investment
Conference, New York, NY. November 6, 2015.
https://www.youtube.com/watch?v=sTIH6ncIXYc.

Musk, Elon. Address at 2016 Tesla Annual Shareholders
Meeting, Mountain View, CA. May 31, 2016. https://www
.youtube.com/watch?v=DvVlNkL8f_0.

World's Worst Demo

Musk, Elon. Address at 2016 Tesla Annual Shareholders
Meeting, Mountain View, CA. May 31, 2016. https://www
.youtube.com/watch?v=DvVlNkL8f_0.

Tesla IPO

Musk, Elon. Interview with Betty Liu. *Bloomberg.* June 29,
2010. https://www.youtube.com/watch?v=QedMgWkhQBk.

Investors and Ideology

Musk, Elon. Interview with Lasse Ladefoged. *Dagbladet
Børsen.* September 23, 2015. https://www.youtube.com
/watch?v=bl5vLC3Xlgc.

Stock Price

Musk, Elon. Interview with Jason Stein. Automotive
News World Congress, Detroit, MI. January 13, 2015.
https://www.youtube.com/watch?v=TK90S7HS3Ng.

Tesla Bailout

Musk, Elon. Address at 2016 Tesla Annual Shareholders
Meeting, Mountain View, CA. May 31, 2016. https://www
.youtube.com/watch?v=DvVlNkL8f_0.

Reality Check

Musk, Elon. Address at 2016 Tesla Annual Shareholders
Meeting, Mountain View, CA. May 31, 2016. https://www
.youtube.com/watch?v=DvVlNkL8f_0.

Don't Cut Corners

Tesla Team. "Response to Mercury News Article, Entitled 'The Hidden Workforce Expanding Tesla's Factory.'" Tesla.com (blog). May 16, 2016. https://www.tesla.com/blog/response-mercury-news-article-hidden-workforce-expanding-teslas-factory.

Building Trust

Musk, Elon. "The House Always Wins." Tesla.com (blog). November 21, 2014. https://www.Tesla.com/blog/house-always-wins.

No Model Years

Musk, Elon. Tesla Motors Q3 2015 earnings call. November 3, 2015. https://www.youtube.com/watch?v=r7YKZ_mV7l4.

8-Year, Infinite Mile Warranty

Musk, Elon. "Infinite Mile Warranty." Tesla.com (blog). August 15, 2014. https://www.Tesla.com/blog/infinite-mile-warranty.

Acquisition of Fremont Factory

Musk, Elon. Interview with Ron Baron. Baron Investment Conference, New York, NY. November 6, 2015. https://www.youtube.com/watch?v=sTIH6ncIXYc.

Fire Risk

Musk, Elon. "The Mission of Tesla." Tesla.com (blog). November 18, 2013. https://www.Tesla.com/blog/mission-tesla.

Range Transparency

Musk, Elon, and Straubel, JB. "Model S Efficiency and Range." Tesla.com (blog). May 9, 2012. https://www.Tesla.com/blog/model-s-efficiency-and-range.

Unprofitability

Musk, Elon. Interview with Betty Liu. *Bloomberg*. June 29, 2010. https://www.youtube.com/watch?v=QedMgWkhQBk.

Deliveries versus Demand

Musk, Elon. Interview with Jason Stein. Automotive News World Congress, Detroit, MI. January 13, 2015. https://www.youtube.com/watch?v=TK90S7HS3Ng.

Supply Chain Woes

Musk, Elon. Interview with Kara Swisher and Walt Mossberg. Code Conference 2016, Rancho Palos Verdes, CA. June 1, 2016. https://www.youtube.com/watch?v=wsixsRI-Sz4.

On Accusations of High Attrition

Musk, Elon. Interview with Jason Stein. Automotive News World Congress, Detroit, MI. January 13, 2015. https://www.youtube.com/watch?v=TK90S7HS3Ng.

Safety

Musk, Elon. Interview with Ron Baron. Baron Investment Conference, New York, NY. November 6, 2015. https://www.youtube.com/watch?v=sTIH6ncIXYc.

Driver Responsibility

Musk, Elon. Interview with Betty Liu. *Bloomberg*. October 10, 2014. https://www.youtube.com/watch?v=Bjq6tXRKfUQ.

Partial Autonomy Now

Musk, Elon. "Master Plan, Part Deux." Tesla.com (blog). July 20, 2016. https://www.tesla.com/blog/master-plan-part-deux.

Autonomous versus Manual Driving

Musk, Elon. Tesla Motors Q1 2016 earnings call. May 4, 2016. https://www.youtube.com/watch?v=0HM7LceSG8Y.

Missing Deadlines

Musk, Elon. Interview with Jason Stein. Automotive News World Congress, Detroit, MI. January 13, 2015. https://www.youtube.com/watch?v=TK90S7HS3Ng.

Musk, Elon. Interview with Kara Swisher and Walt Mossberg. Code Conference 2016, Rancho Palos Verdes, CA. June 1, 2016. https://www.youtube.com/watch?v=wsixsRI-Sz4.

Creating Deadlines

Musk, Elon. Tesla Motors Q1 2016 earnings call. May 4, 2016.
https://www.youtube.com/watch?v=oHM7LceSG8Y.

Mission

Musk, Elon. "The Mission of Tesla." Tesla.com (blog).
November 18, 2013. https://www.Tesla.com/blog/mission
-tesla.

Low Volume, High Price (Roadster)

Musk, Elon. Presentation at Model 3 unveiling event,
Hawthorne, CA. March 31, 2016. https://www.youtube
.com/watch?v=38hQr9zxcLs.

Mid Volume, Less-High Price (Model S)

Musk, Elon. Presentation at Model 3 unveiling event,
Hawthorne, CA. March 31, 2016. https://www.youtube
.com/watch?v=38hQr9zxcLs.

Mid Volume, Less-High Price (Model X)

Musk, Elon. Presentation at Model 3 unveiling event,
Hawthorne, CA. March 31, 2016. https://www.youtube
.com/watch?v=38hQr9zxcLs.

High Volume, Affordable Price (Model 3)

Musk, Elon. Presentation at Model 3 unveiling event,
Hawthorne, CA. March 31, 2016. https://www.youtube
.com/watch?v=38hQr9zxcLs.

Model 3 Preorders

Musk, Elon. Interview with Kara Swisher and Walt Mossberg.
Code Conference 2016, Rancho Palos Verdes, CA. June 1,
2016. https://www.youtube.com/watch?v=wsixsRI-Sz4.

Tesla Energy

Tesla Energy press kit. Tesla.com. April 30, 2015. https://www
.tesla.com/presskit/teslaenergy?via=newsletter&source
=CSAMedition.

Next Generation of Tesla Stationary Power Storage
Musk, Elon. Tesla Motors Q2 2016 earnings call. August 3, 2016. https://www.youtube.com/watch?v=Ooo7tHQe-yo.

Gigafactory
Musk, Elon. Interview with Ron Baron. Baron Investment Conference, New York, NY. November 6, 2015. https://www.youtube.com/watch?v=sTIH6ncIXYc.
Musk, Elon. Remarks at Gigafactory grand opening, Sparks, NV. July 29, 2016. https://www.tesla.com/videos/tesla-gigafactory-grand-opening.

Lithium Ion Batteries
Musk, Elon. Interview with Kara Swisher and Walt Mossberg. Code Conference 2016, Rancho Palos Verdes, CA. June 1, 2016. https://www.youtube.com/watch?v=wsixsRI-Sz4.

Recycling Batteries
Musk, Elon. Interview with Margaret Leinen. American Geophysical Union Fall Meeting Presidential Forum, San Francisco, CA. December 15, 2015. https://www.youtube.com/watch?v=b2LCK9dw9as.

Tesla Watch
Musk, Elon. "Announcing the Tesla Model W." Tesla.com (blog). April 1, 2015. https://www.Tesla.com/blog/announcing-tesla-model-w.

Apple
Musk, Elon. Twitter post. October 9, 2015, 3:03 p.m. https://twitter.com/elonmusk/status/652605371857530880.

Bioweapon Defense Mode
Musk, Elon. Presentation at Model X unveiling event, Fremont, CA. September 29, 2015. https://www.youtube.com/watch?v=RUz_EXSmp9w.

Ludicrous Mode

Heath, Chris. "How Elon Musk Plans on Reinventing the World (and Mars)." *GQ*. December 12, 2015. http://www .gq.com/story/elon-musk-mars-spacex-tesla-interview.

Open-Source Patents

Musk, Elon. "All Our Patent Are Belong to You." Tesla.com (blog). June 12, 2014. https://www.Tesla.com/blog/all-our -patent-are-belong-you.

Musk, Elon. "All Our Patent Are Belong to You." Tesla.com (blog). June 12, 2014. https://www.Tesla.com/blog/all-our -patent-are-belong-you.

Zero-Emission Credits

Musk, Elon. Interview with Jason Stein. Automotive News World Congress, Detroit, MI. January 13, 2015. https://www.youtube.com/watch?v=TK90S7HS3Ng.

Retail Locations

Musk, Elon. "The Tesla Approach to Distributing and Servicing Cars." Tesla.com (blog). October 22, 2012. https://www.Tesla.com/blog/tesla-approach-distributing- and-servicing-cars.

Sales Philosophy

Musk, Elon. "The Tesla Approach to Distributing and Servicing Cars." Tesla.com (blog). October 22, 2012. https://www.Tesla.com/blog/tesla-approach-distributing -and-servicing-cars.

Service Philosophy

Musk, Elon. "Creating the World's Best Service and Warranty Program." Tesla.com (blog). April 26, 2013. https://www .Tesla.com/blog/creating-world%E2%80%99s-best-service -and-warranty-program-0.

Musk, Elon. "To the People of New Jersey." Tesla.com (blog). March 14, 2014. https://www.tesla.com/blog/people-new -jersey.

Pitfalls of Auto Dealers

Musk, Elon. "The Tesla Approach to Distributing and Servicing Cars." Tesla.com (blog). October 22, 2012. https://www.Tesla.com/blog/tesla-approach-distributing -and-servicing-cars.

Potential Auto Dealer Partnerships

Musk, Elon. Interview with Jason Stein. Automotive News World Congress, Detroit, MI. January 13, 2015. https://www.youtube.com/watch?v=TK9oS7HS3Ng.

Focus

Musk, Elon. Address at 2015 Tesla Annual Shareholders Meeting, Mountain View, CA. June 9, 2015. https://www .youtube.com/watch?v=Q6oFOIV6Ew8.

1 Million Cars by 2020

Musk, Elon. Tesla Motors Q1 2016 earnings call. May 4, 2016. https://www.youtube.com/watch?v=0HM7LceSG8Y.

ENVIRONMENTALISM AND SUSTAINABLE ENERGY

Geosciences

Musk, Elon. Interview with Margaret Leinen. American Geophysical Union Fall Meeting Presidential Forum, San Francisco, CA. December 15, 2015. https://www.youtube .com/watch?v=b2LCK9dw9as.

Climate Change

Hoffman, Carl. "Elon Musk, the Rocket Man with a Sweet Ride." *Smithsonian* magazine. December 2012. http://www .smithsonianmag.com/science-nature/elon-musk-the -rocket-man-with-a-sweet-ride-136059680/?no-ist.

Musk, Elon. Interview with Alison van Diggelen. Computer History Museum Revolutionaries, Mountain View, CA. January 22, 2013. https://www.youtube.com/watch?v =AHHwXUm3iI.

Elon Does Not Hate Hydrocarbons

Musk, Elon. Interview at Offshore Northern Seas, Stavanger, Norway. August 2014. https://www.youtube.com/watch?v=oZsVxSDB7NY.

Future of Oil and Gas

Musk, Elon. Interview at Offshore Northern Seas, Stavanger, Norway. August 2014. https://www.youtube.com/watch?v=oZsVxSDB7NY.

Musk, Elon. Interview at Offshore Northern Seas, Stavanger, Norway. August 2014. https://www.youtube.com/watch?v=oZsVxSDB7NY.

Transition from Fossil Fuels

Davis, Johnny. "One More Giant Leap." The *Telegraph*. August 4, 2007. http://www.telegraph.co.uk/culture/3666994/One-more-giant-leap.html.

Conservation

Musk, Elon. Presentation at Université Paris 1 Panthéon-Sorbonne, Paris, France. December 2, 2015. https://www.youtube.com/watch?v=iavquu6PP9g.

Best and Worst Cases of Delaying Transition to Sustainable Energy

Musk, Elon. Presentation at Université Paris 1 Panthéon-Sorbonne, Paris, France. December 2, 2015. https://www.youtube.com/watch?v=iavquu6PP9g.

De Facto Gasoline Subsidies

Musk, Elon. Address at 2016 Tesla Annual Shareholders Meeting, Mountain View, CA. May 31, 2016. https://www.youtube.com/watch?v=DvVlNkL8f_o.

Carbon Tax

Musk, Elon. Interview with Alison van Diggelen. Computer History Museum Revolutionaries, Mountain View, CA. January 22, 2013. https://www.youtube.com/watch?v=AHHwXUm3iI.

Carbon Tax Opponents

Musk, Elon. Presentation at Université Paris 1 Panthéon-Sorbonne, Paris, France. December 2, 2015. https://www.youtube.com/watch?v=iavquu6PP9g.

Solar Power

Musk, Elon. "Elon Musk: The Mind Behind Tesla, SpaceX, SolarCity. . . ." TED Talk, Long Beach, CA. February 27, 2013. https://www.ted.com/talks/elon_musk_the_mind_behind_tesla_spacex_solarcity.

Musk, Elon. Interview at Offshore Northern Seas, Stavanger, Norway. August 2014. https://www.youtube.com/watch?v=oZsVxSDB7NY.

China's Progress with Solar Panels

Musk, Elon. Interview with Chris Anderson. South by Southwest Conference, Austin, TX. March 9, 2013. https://www.youtube.com/watch?v=LeQMWdOMa-A.

The Hard Part of Solar Power

Musk, Elon. Interview with Chris Anderson. South by Southwest Conference, Austin, TX. March 9, 2013. https://www.youtube.com/watch?v=LeQMWdOMa-A.

SolarCity

Musk, Elon. Interview with Chris Anderson. South by Southwest Conference, Austin, TX. March 9, 2013. https://www.youtube.com/watch?v=LeQMWdOMa-A.

SolarCity Acquisition

Musk, Elon. "Master Plan, Part Deux." Tesla.com (blog). July 20, 2016. https://www.tesla.com/blog/master-plan-part-deux.

Musk, Elon. Press teleconference on Tesla acquisition of SolarCity. June 22, 2016. https://www.youtube.com/watch?v=KUTRQavXMK4.

Musk, Elon. Press teleconference on Tesla acquisition of SolarCity. June 22, 2016. https://www.youtube.com/watch?v=KUTRQavXMK4.

What the World Needs

Musk, Elon. Press teleconference on Tesla acquisition of SolarCity. June 22, 2016. https://www.youtube.com/watch?v=KUTRQavXMK4.

What People Can Do

Musk, Elon. Presentation at Université Paris 1 Panthéon-Sorbonne, Paris, France. December 2, 2015. https://www.youtube.com/watch?v=iavquu6PP9g.

Musk, Elon. Presentation at Université Paris 1 Panthéon-Sorbonne, Paris, France. December 2, 2015. https://www.youtube.com/watch?v=iavquu6PP9g.

SPACEX

A Small Fortune

Lemley, Brad. "Shooting the Moon: Elon Musk Bets His Entire Fortune on a Rocket." *Discover* magazine. September 8, 2005. http://discovermagazine.com/2005/sep/cover.

Idea for SpaceX

Musk, Elon. Interview with Sal Khan. Khan Academy Chats, Mountain View, CA. April 17, 2013. https://www.khanacademy.org/talks-and-interviews/khan-academy-living-room-chats/v/elon-musk.

Mars Oasis

Anderson, Chris. "Elon Musk's Mission to Mars." *Wired*. October 21, 2012. http://www.wired.com/2012/10/ff-elon-musk-qa/.

A Nation of Explorers

Musk, Elon. Interview with Chris Anderson. South by Southwest Conference, Austin, TX. March 9, 2013. https://www.youtube.com/watch?v=LeQMWdOMa-A.

Reducing the Cost of Spaceflight

Anderson, Chris. "Elon Musk's Mission to Mars." *Wired.*
    October 21, 2012. http://www.wired.com/2012/10/ff-elon
    -musk-qa/.

Musk, Elon. Interview with Alison van Diggelen. Computer
    History Museum Revolutionaries, Mountain View, CA.
    January 22, 2013. https://www.youtube.com/watch?v
    =AHHwXUm3iI.

The Goal of SpaceX

Musk, Elon. "RE: SPACE." *hitRECord on TV.* Pivot. February 1,
    2014. https://www.youtube.com/watch?v=hwMIAKabRng.

Historical Context

Strauss, Robert. "The Next, Next Thing." *Pennsylvania
    Gazette.* November 4, 2008. http://www.upenn.edu
    /gazette/1108/feature4_1.html.

Reasons to Make Life Multiplanetary

Musk, Elon. Interview with Margaret Leinen. American
    Geophysical Union Fall Meeting Presidential Forum, San
    Francisco, CA. December 15, 2015. https://www.youtube
    .com/watch?v=b2LCK9dw9as.

Musk, Elon. Press conference on SpaceX's commitment
    to develop fully reusable rockets, Washington, DC.
    September 29, 2011. https://www.youtube.com
    /watch?v=qbItNdHi2tg.

Success

Corsello, Andrew. "The Believer." *GQ.* December 31, 2008.
    http://www.gq.com/story/elon-musk-paypal-solar-power
    -electric-cars-space-travel.

First Order of Business

Hoffman, Carl. "Elon Musk, the Rocket Man with a Sweet
    Ride." *Smithsonian* magazine. December 2012. http://www
    .smithsonianmag.com/science-nature/elon-musk-the
    -rocket-man-with-a-sweet-ride-136059680/?no-ist.

Problems with Aerospace Firms

Anderson, Chris. "Elon Musk's Mission to Mars." *Wired*. October 21, 2012. http://www.wired.com/2012/10/ff-elon -musk-qa/.

Anderson, Chris. "Elon Musk's Mission to Mars." *Wired*. October 21, 2012. http://www.wired.com/2012/10/ff-elon -musk-qa/.

Cost versus Reliability

Reingold, Jennifer. "Hondas in Space." *Fast Company*. February 1, 2005. http://www.fastcompany.com/52065 /hondas-space.

Competing in Space

Anderson, Chris. "Elon Musk's Mission to Mars." *Wired*. October 21, 2012. http://www.wired.com/2012/10/ff-elon -musk-qa/.

Competitive Advantage

Musk, Elon. Interview with Jaime Peraire. Massachusetts Institute of Technology Aeronautics and Astronautics Centennial Symposium, Cambridge, MA. October 24, 2014. https://www.youtube.com/watch?v=PULkWGHeIQQ.

Aerospace versus Commercial Suppliers

Musk, Elon. Speech at International Space Development Conference. Los Angeles, CA. May 4, 2006. https://www .youtube.com/watch?v=1mWfelh28wg.

Blue Origin, Boeing, and Lockheed Partnership

Musk, Elon. "Elon Musk on the Next Step for SpaceX, Nevada Gigafactory." *Countdown to the Closing Bell*. Fox Business Network. September 17, 2014. https://www .youtube.com/watch?v=ASrw-NdtchQ.

Boeing versus SpaceX

Musk, Elon. Interview with Rachel Crane. *CNNMoney*. September 18, 2014. http://money.cnn.com/video /news/2014/09/18/elon-musk-spacex-boeing-nasa .cnnmoney/.

Jeff Bezos in Space

Musk, Elon. Interview with Chris Anderson. South by
Southwest Conference, Austin, TX. March 9, 2013.
https://www.youtube.com/watch?v=LeQMWdOMa-A.

Launch Day

Musk, Elon. Interview with Max Chafkin. Inc. 5000
Conference, National Harbor, MD. 2008. https://www
.youtube.com/watch?v=Xcut1JfTMoM.

Falcon 1

David, Leonard. "SpaceX Private Rocket Shifts to Island
Launch." Space.com. August 12, 2005. http://www.space
.com/1422-spacex-private-rocket-shifts-island-launch
.html.

Naming Booster Stages

Musk, Elon. Interview with John Doerr. Google Zeitgeist '08.
September 18, 2008. https://www.youtube.com/watch?v
=KzNPaBVFzWc.

Simplicity

Lemley, Brad. "Shooting the Moon: Elon Musk Bets
His Entire Fortune on a Rocket." *Discover* magazine.
September 8, 2005. http://discovermagazine.com/2005
/sep/cover.

On Not Reaching Orbit

Musk, Elon. Interview with Max Chafkin. Inc. 5000
Conference, National Harbor, MD. 2008. https://www
.youtube.com/watch?v=Xcut1JfTMoM.
Hoffman, Carl. "Now 0-for-3, SpaceX's Elon Musk Vows to
Make Orbit." *Wired*. August 5, 2008. http://www.wired
.com/2008/08/musk-qa/.

Falcon 1 Flight 4

Musk, Elon. Address to SpaceX employees after Falcon 1
Flight 4, Hawthorne, CA. September 28, 2008.
https://www.youtube.com/watch?v=5pbrO16WTrg.

New US Space Strategy

Musk, Elon. "What's in the Stars for NASA?" *Science Friday*. NPR. April 16, 2010. http://www.npr.org/templates/story /story.php?storyId=126049674.

Importance of Pushing Forward

Musk, Elon. Interview with Michael Suffredini. International Space Station Research and Development Conference, Boston, MA. July 7, 2015. https://www.youtube.com /watch?v=hJDoMMP4nkM.

First Rocket Landing

Musk, Elon. Interview with Sal Khan. Khan Academy Chats, Mountain View, CA. April 17, 2013. https://www .khanacademy.org/talks-and-interviews/khan-academy -living-room-chats/v/elon-musk.

RUD

Musk, Elon. Twitter post. June 15, 2016, 8:07 a.m. https://twitter.com/elonmusk/status/743097668725940225.

Reusable Rockets

SpaceX News. "X Marks the Spot: Falcon 9 Attempts Ocean Platform Landing." SpaceX.com. December 16, 2014. http://www.spacex.com/news/2014/12/16/x-marks-spot -falcon-9-attempts-ocean-platform-landing.

Musk, Elon. Press conference on SpaceX's commitment to develop fully reusable rockets, Washington, DC. September 29, 2011. https://www.youtube.com/watch?v =qbItNdHi2tg.

The Expense of Expendable Booster Stages

Musk, Elon. Interview with Kara Swisher and Walt Mossberg. Code Conference 2016, Rancho Palos Verdes, CA. June 1, 2016. https://www.youtube.com/watch?v=wsixsRI-Sz4.

Reaction to First Vertical Landing

Musk, Elon. Press teleconference after first vertical landing. December 21, 2015. https://www.youtube.com/watch?v=K31EJHnrm-E.

Musk, Elon. Press teleconference after first vertical landing. December 21, 2015. https://www.youtube.com/watch?v=K31EJHnrm-E.

Reaction to First Vertical Landing at Sea

Musk, Elon. SpaceX Dragon CRS-8 post-launch news conference. Cape Canaveral, FL. April 8, 2016. https://www.youtube.com/watch?v=HEjC7swudhk.

Taking SpaceX Public

Musk, Elon. Interview with Alison van Diggelen. Computer History Museum Revolutionaries, Mountain View, CA. January 22, 2013. https://www.youtube.com/watch?v=AHHwXUm3iI.

Air Force EELV Block Buy

Musk, Elon. Press conference after Falcon 9's successful ocean landing. Washington, DC. April 14, 2014. https://www.youtube.com/watch?v=wYNtDOmPUao.

Transferring Cargo to and from ISS

Musk, Elon. Interview with Fred Hochberg. Export-Import Bank Annual Conference, Washington, DC. April 25, 2014. https://www.youtube.com/watch?v=rGsLm1XR3bE.

Designing Space Suits

Musk, Elon. Interview with Michael Suffredini. International Space Station Research and Development Conference, Boston, MA. July 7, 2015. https://www.youtube.com/watch?v=hJD0MMP4nkM.

Dragon V2

Musk, Elon. Interview with Kara Swisher and Walt Mossberg. Code Conference 2016, Rancho Palos Verdes, CA. June 1, 2016. https://www.youtube.com/watch?v=wsixsRI-Sz4.

Disagreements with NASA

Heath, Chris. "How Elon Musk Plans on Reinventing the World (and Mars)." *GQ*. December 12, 2015. http://www.gq.com/story/elon-musk-mars-spacex-tesla-interview.

The Improbable

Musk, Elon. Video at Living Legends of Aviation awards dinner, Beverly Hills, CA. January 22, 2010. https://www.youtube.com/watch?v=QXH-puBE10Q.

A New Frontier

Musk, Elon. Presentation at the International Astronautical Congress, Guadalajara, Mexico. September 27, 2016. https://www.youtube.com/watch?v=10gECHeMSds.

ENGINEERING, DESIGN, AND MANUFACTURE

Start in Engineering

Anderson, Chris. "Elon Musk's Mission to Mars." *Wired*. October 21, 2012. http://www.wired.com/2012/10/ff-elon-musk-qa/.

Favorite Part of the Job

Musk, Elon. Video at Living Legends of Aviation awards dinner, Beverly Hills, CA. January 22, 2010. https://www.youtube.com/watch?v=QXH-puBE10Q.

Engineering Is Magic

Elliott, Hannah. "At Home with Elon Musk: The (Soon-to-Be) Bachelor Billionaire." *Forbes*. March 26, 2012. http://www.forbes.com/sites/hannahelliott/2012/03/26/at-home-with-elon-musk-the-soon-to-be-bachelor-billionaire/#6d404b524ead.

Engineers Should Have Kids

Musk, Elon. Interview with Sarah Lacy. The Founder Showcase, Mountain View, CA. August 3, 2010. https://www.youtube.com/watch?v=lNpd8wzDCEc.

Immigration Laws

Musk, Elon. Interview with Fred Hochberg. Export-Import Bank Annual Conference, Washington, DC. April 25, 2014. https://www.youtube.com/watch?v=rGsLm1XR3bE&list.

Design and Aesthetics

Musk, Elon. Interview with Steve Jurvetson. Stanford Technology Ventures Program Future Fest, Stanford University, Stanford, CA. October 7, 2015. https://www.youtube.com/watch?v=Zos-y4VJsdk.

Achieving Perfection

Musk, Elon. Interview with Kristie Lu Stout. StartmeupHK Venture Forum, Hong Kong. January 26, 2016. https://www.youtube.com/watch?v=jiRLGpm5CiY.

Details

Musk, Elon. Interview with Steve Jurvetson. Stanford Technology Ventures Program Future Fest, Stanford University, Stanford, CA. October 7, 2015. https://www.youtube.com/watch?v=Zos-y4VJsdk.

The Challenge of Manufacturing

Musk, Elon. Address at 2016 Tesla Annual Shareholders Meeting, Mountain View, CA. May 31, 2016. https://www.youtube.com/watch?v=DvVlNkL8f_0.

Believe in Manufacturing

Musk, Elon. Tesla Motors Q1 2016 earnings call. May 4, 2016. https://www.youtube.com/watch?v=0HM7LceSG8Y.

Model 3 Design

Musk, Elon. Tesla Motors Q1 2016 earnings call. May 4, 2016. https://www.youtube.com/watch?v=0HM7LceSG8Y.

Building the Tesla Factory

Musk, Elon. Address at 2016 Tesla Annual Shareholders Meeting, Mountain View, CA. May 31, 2016. https://www.youtube.com/watch?v=DvVlNkL8f_0.

172

ROCKET MAN

Musk, Elon. Address at 2016 Tesla Annual Shareholders Meeting, Mountain View, CA. May 31, 2016. https://www.youtube.com/watch?v=DvVlNkL8f_0.

Alien Dreadnought
Musk, Elon. Tesla Motors Q2 2016 earnings call. August 3, 2016. https://www.youtube.com/watch?v=Ooo7tHQe-yo.

Bidirectional Feedback Loop
Musk, Elon. Interview with Fred Hochberg. Export-Import Bank Annual Conference, Washington, DC. April 25, 2014. https://www.youtube.com/watch?v=rGsLm1XR3bE.

WEALTH AND MONEY

Eggs in One Basket
Chafkin, Max. "Entrepreneur of the Year, 2007: Elon Musk." *Inc.* December 1, 2007. http://www.inc.com/magazine/20071201/entrepreneur-of-the-year-elon-musk.html.

Choosing a Venture Capitalist
Musk, Elon. Interview with Sarah Lacy. PandoMonthly: Fireside Chat with Elon Musk, Santa Monica, CA. July 12, 2012. https://www.youtube.com/watch?v=uegOUmgKB4E.

Investing Your Own Money
Musk, Elon. Interview with Sarah Lacy. PandoMonthly: Fireside Chat with Elon Musk, Santa Monica, CA. July 12, 2012. https://www.youtube.com/watch?v=uegOUmgKB4E.
Musk, Elon. Address at 2016 Tesla Annual Shareholders Meeting, Mountain View, CA. May 31, 2016. https://www.youtube.com/watch?v=DvVlNkL8f_0.

Judging Achievement
Musk, Elon. "Elon Musk and the Frontier of Technology." *Think Tank.* PBS. December 13, 2007. http://www.pbs.org/thinktank/transcript1292.html.

Giving Away Assets
Musk, Elon. Interview with Alison van Diggelen. Computer
    History Museum Revolutionaries, Mountain View, CA.
    January 22, 2013. https://www.youtube.com/watch?v
    =AHHwXUm3iI.

Hopes for Children
Davis, Johnny. "One More Giant Leap." The *Telegraph*.
    August 4, 2007. http://www.telegraph.co.uk/culture
    /3666994/One-more-giant-leap.html.

LIFE LESSONS

Enjoy Your Work
Strauss, Robert. "The Next, Next Thing." *Pennsylvania
    Gazette*. November 4, 2008. http://www.upenn.edu
    /gazette/1108/feature4_1.html.

Burning Man Epiphanies
Musk, Elon. Interview with Alison van Diggelen. Computer
    History Museum Revolutionaries, Mountain View, CA.
    January 22, 2013. https://www.youtube.com/watch?v
    =AHHwXUm3iI.

Turning Possibility into Probability
Junod, Tom. "Elon Musk: Triumph of His Will." *Esquire*.
    November 14, 2012. http://www.esquire.com
    /news-politics/a16681/elon-musk-interview-1212/.

Just Be Yourself
Musk, Elon. Twitter post. December 20, 2014, 3:42 p.m.
    https://twitter.com/elonmusk/status/546450680689356800.
Musk, Elon. Twitter post. December 20, 2014, 3:55 p.m.
    https://twitter.com/elonmusk/status/546453860936474625.

Long-Term Grudges

Chafkin, Max. "Entrepreneur of the Year, 2007: Elon Musk."
Inc. December 1, 2007. http://www.inc.com/magazine
/20071201/entrepreneur-of-the-year-elon-musk.html.

Fear

Musk, Elon. "Elon Musk Gets Introspective." AutoBild.tv.
November 6, 2014. https://www.youtube.com/watch?v
=IooquUJmM9M.

Musk, Elon. Interview with Sam Altman. Y Combinator's
"How to Build the Future" series, Fremont, CA.
September 15, 2016. https://www.youtube.com
/watch?v=tnBQmEqBCY0.

Naysayers

Musk, Elon. Tesla Motors Q1 2016 earnings call. May 4, 2016.
https://www.youtube.com/watch?v=oHM7LceSG8Y.

New York Times Controversy

Musk, Elon. "A Most Peculiar Test Drive." Tesla.com (blog).
February 13, 2013. https://www.Tesla.com/blog/most
-peculiar-test-drive.

Critical Reviews

Musk, Elon. Interview with Chris Anderson. South by
Southwest Conference, Austin, TX. March 9, 2013.
https://www.youtube.com/watch?v=LeQMWdOMa-A.

Physics and the Universe

Musk, Elon. Twitter post. February 16, 2016, 1:39 p.m.
https://twitter.com/elonmusk/status/699709623406702592.

Sleep

Musk, Elon. Interview with Alison van Diggelen. Computer
History Museum Revolutionaries, Mountain View, CA.
January 22, 2013. https://www.youtube.com/watch?v
=AHHwXUm3iI.

Take Risks While Young
Musk, Elon. Commencement address at the University of
    Southern California, Los Angeles, CA. May 16, 2014.
    https://www.youtube.com/watch?v=DYN_0EIQj4s.

Waiting for Godot
Musk, Elon. Twitter post. April 17, 2016, 2:38 p.m.
    https://twitter.com/elonmusk/status/721815145932951552.

Work-Life Balance
Musk, Elon. Interview with Kara Swisher and Walt Mossberg.
    Code Conference 2016, Rancho Palos Verdes, CA. June 1,
    2016. https://www.youtube.com/watch?v=wsixsRI-Sz4.

Credit Where It's Due
Musk, Elon. Conversation with Bill Gates. Boao Forum for
    Asia, Boao, China. March 29, 2015. https://www.youtube
    .com/watch?v=TRpjhIhpuiU.

Trying
Musk, Elon. "Fast Cars and Rocket Ships." *60 Minutes*. CBS.
    March 30, 2014. http://www.cbsnews.com/news/tesla
    -and-spacex-elon-musks-industrial-empire/.

Convincing the Public
Musk, Elon. Interview with Steve Jurvetson. Stanford
    Technology Ventures Program Future Fest, Stanford
    University, Stanford, CA. October 7, 2015. https://www
    .youtube.com/watch?v=Zos-y4VJsdk.

Stay Focused
Musk, Elon. Address at 2016 Tesla Annual Shareholders
    Meeting, Mountain View, CA. May 31, 2016. https://www
    .youtube.com/watch?v=DvVlNkL8f_0.

Legacy
Heath, Chris. "How Elon Musk Plans on Reinventing the
    World (and Mars)." *GQ*. December 12, 2015. http://www
    .gq.com/story/elon-musk-mars-spacex-tesla-interview.